PRAISE FOR *FLIGI* AND BARBARA BELL

"As one of my Navy Test Pilot School instructors, Barb taught me an important lesson about communicating well—one that I have carried with me throughout my career. Now in *Flight Lessons* she shares her lessons with you. As someone who has experienced Barb as a superior, instructor, colleague, and friend, I must say that this book accurately and definitively describes what it is like to be 'one of the only' or 'the only one' at USNA and in the naval service, and how to learn from and succeed in a challenging environment. Her lessons learned will truly benefit all who are willing to read and listen. I recommend it for all who wish to become a better leader!"

—Captain Robert Curbeam
US Navy (ret); former astronaut

"Barb's story in *Flight Lessons* is as enlightening, entertaining, and educational to me today as a business executive as it would be to my daughter as a young fashion merchandising major. Her hard-learned life lessons are spot on, and relevant to anyone trying to chart their life's flight path: 'Find your own wings'; 'When you don't fit in, choose to stand out'; 'We must tell our stories if we are going to continue to move the needle.' It's a great read and gets two huge thumbs up from me."

—Captain Russ Bartlett
US Navy (ret); former commanding officer and flight leader, Navy Blue Angels

"*Flight Lessons* is a powerful life story of courage and fortitude: 'Grit'; 'Life is full of hills'; 'Don't shy away from those challenges.' Barb's story is packed with inspiring lessons for leaders at every career level. Barb thoughtfully takes on the important and real topic of gender bias. This book is a must-read for both civilian and military leadership curricula. Once I started reading, I was motivated to go 'summit every hill.'"

—Craig Faller
Admiral, US Navy (ret); former commander of US Southern Command

"Few corporate leaders and even fewer professionals have the grit, determination, intellect, and zeal to succeed when the odds are stacked against them. Instead, Captain Bell thrived on adversity, impasse, and barriers. At a time when the rights of citizens are marred by discrimination from race and gender, Barbara answers the call to change the dialogue with unquestioned credentials and unequaled merit. Her flight path, *Flight Lessons*, serves not only as an inspiration to young women but also to all of those who wish to Fly High in life. She is an inspiration, a pioneer, a mentor and, most importantly, a grace-filled leader."

—Greg Glaros
CEO, SYNEXXUS INC.

"How we calculate educational opportunities and disrupt inequities, cultivate personal resilience and promote resolve, and recognize how role models matter—these 'gritting it out' challenges anchor a new book by Dr. Barbara Bell—an educator, former naval officer, and Navy aviator-pioneer who writes with compelling nuance, 'This is why I tell my story.' This riveting narrative is a biographical blend of elegant prose and candid accounts of Bell's glass-ceiling-shattering exploits in education, aviation, and the workplace. This book confronts the complexities of gender, race, and sense of place across a canvas of power and privilege. Bell's wise and sometimes wistful unwrapping of 'life lessons' should engage scholars and school leaders, STEM teachers and university officials, policymakers and business leaders, citizens and elected officials, along with students and parents, in an immensely gratifying and uplifting journey toward 'finding our wings.'"

—Claire Smrekar, PhD
Vanderbilt University

"Having known Barb Bell for years and flying in sister squadrons in the Navy, it was a pleasure to read about some of her experiences—long before we met flying airplanes. Barb takes us on a tour of the Naval Academy's beginning in coed education. It was tough. Leadership was the key—it always is—to making life better or worse.

"Barb pulls back some of the curtains on how it was to be a pioneer at places like the US Naval Academy when senior leadership in the Navy had not come to the same conclusion Congress had on the matter. Women were allowed, yes, but not quite welcome, not quite yet. The tenacity and strength that she and her classmates had to have is a beautiful testimony to their determination to stand and fight, and not just for themselves. Their dreams really were just the starting pistols in the journey of this league of extraordinary gentlewomen."

—Captain Tammie Jo Shults

Navy pilot; SWA captain (ret); author of Nerves of Steel

"I could not stop reading once I began. Thought-provoking, introspection-inspiring, and memory-awakening, I could hear Barb speak these words as I read. Her voice is that clear. I want to show it to my colleagues at work—the young women especially—to inspire them to reach for the stars. It is an easy yet inspiring read; I can't wait for it to be released."

—Dori Freer

Captain, US Navy (ret); former commander, Defense Contract Management Agency at Sikorsky Aircraft; Navy helicopter pilot; USNA 1982

"As a woman of color, Dr. Bell's book *Flight Lessons* felt like a different version of my life. I know now why she is the strong, independent, 'always learning' woman I have known and admired for over fifteen years. Her book is heartfelt and authentic yet full of practical advice. Her words of wisdom are not just for women but for anyone who wants a front seat in this game of life where we can label a challenge a hindrance or a stepping stone. I would encourage every teacher to read the book, then buy copies for their students and every mom to do the same for their daughter."

—Bonnie Wilson, DHA, MBA, BSN, RN, NEA-BC

Xceeding the Mark, LLC, Executive Coaching & Consulting

"Barb's story is a testament to the power of trusting oneself, the greatest hurdle we must overcome to occupy the spaces that were not designed for our occupancy. Detailing her disciplined upbringing in a small Michigan town to becoming a standout at the United States Naval Academy, despite the interminable gender discrimination to which she was often subjected, to navigating an array of subsequent triumphs and challenges, Barb writes with a clarity that meets each reader where they are while also challenging them to walk in their own power. Yes, it is unequivocally true that Barb is an accomplished naval officer, aviator, and Navy captain. But any mention of these accolades must also include the titles *bold*, *driven*, and *survivor*. Among other things, *Flight Lessons* wields the power of language and personal narrative to move readers from one place in their lives to the next."

—MarQuis L. Chappell
Director of equity and inclusion, Upper School English Faculty, the Harpeth Hall School

"Barbara Bell was inspired to take to the sky as a Captain in the United States Navy by the trailblazing example of Amelia Earhart and other women pioneers in aviation. But even more importantly, she was inspired by Earhart's advice to "build a runway" for those who are following after her. With *Flight Lessons*, she does just that. By recounting and reflecting upon her own educational and career trajectory, Barb gives readers—especially young women—important life advice for navigating the vast expanse that is the future. This book is an honest and hopeful account of how to identify, stay true to, and realize your dreams. Barb gives real-life testimony to the idea that obstacles are not only surmountable, but they also can build your resolve and help you forge the life you want to lead. In no uncertain terms, she makes one thing clear to determined young women everywhere: If you can dream it, you can do it."

—Megan K. Murphy
Executive Director, National Coalition of Girls' Schools

"A warrior and hero, Barb's voice will resonate strongly and clearly with those wishing to soar. Her compelling guidance, illustrated through personal accounts and good humor, lay an essential foundation for success."

—Allison Webster-Giddings
Captain, US Navy (ret), Ed.D., Navy Test Pilot, Professor of Engineering, US Naval Academy

FLIGHT LESSONS

NAVIGATING THROUGH LIFE'S TURBULENCE
AND LEARNING TO FLY HIGH

FLIGHT LESSONS

NAVIGATING THROUGH LIFE'S TURBULENCE
AND LEARNING TO FLY HIGH

BARBARA BELL

Published by Advantage, Charleston, South Carolina.
Member of Advantage Media Group.

ADVANTAGE is a registered trademark, and the Advantage colophon is a trademark of Advantage Media Group, Inc.

Printed in the United States of America.

10 9 8 7 6 5 4 3 2 1

ISBN: 978-1-64225-360-3
LCCN: 2021924931

Book design by Mary Hamilton.
Front cover photo by Judith Hill Photography.

This publication is designed to provide accurate and authoritative information in regard to the subject matter covered. It is sold with the understanding that the publisher is not engaged in rendering legal, accounting, or other professional services. If legal advice or other expert assistance is required, the services of a competent professional person should be sought.

Advantage Media Group is proud to be a part of the Tree Neutral® program. Tree Neutral offsets the number of trees consumed in the production and printing of this book by taking proactive steps such as planting trees in direct proportion to the number of trees used to print books. To learn more about Tree Neutral, please visit **www.treeneutral.com**.

Advantage Media Group is a publisher of business, self-improvement, and professional development books and online learning. We help entrepreneurs, business leaders, and professionals share their Stories, Passion, and Knowledge to help others Learn & Grow. Do you have a manuscript or book idea that you would like us to consider for publishing? Please visit **advantagefamily.com**.

To Millie and Karen—my "sisters" who learned to fly each in their own way. And to my daughter, Kim Anh, who is finding her wings.

CONTENTS

WHY I TELL MY STORY 1

PART ONE: 9
GRITTING IT OUT

DREAMS OF FLYING. 11

POSSIBILITIES 13

PLEBE SUMMER 19

DEFENDING OUR PRESENCE 25

SISTERS, WE THREE. 31

BUILDING OUR RESISTANCE 39

LEAN INTO THE HILLS 47

FINDING OURSELVES. 51

STAND UP AND SPEAK OUT 57

EYE ON THE PRIZE 61

BRIDGE TO THE FUTURE 67

LAUNCH! 73

FIND YOUR WINGS 77

PART TWO: **81**

NAVIGATING TURBULENCE

STRAP IN 83

DON'T SKIP FLIGHT SCHOOL 85

"NO" IS A COMPLETE SENTENCE 89

GO DEEPER ... THEN SURFACE 93

GEAR UP 99

OTHERS ARE WATCHING 103

AVERAGE WON'T CUT IT 107

GIFTS OFTEN COME IN UNEXPECTED PACKAGES . . . 111

WINGS OF GOLD 115

PUSH ON
DESPITE THE NAYSAYERS 121

FLYING HIGH 127

FIND YOUR WINGS 133

PART THREE: 137

EARNING YOUR WINGS

SQUARE YOUR SHOULDERS. 139

PAST, PRESENT…. 143

… AND FUTURE. 149

STEP OUT ON FAITH 153

DON'T CLIP
YOUR OWN WINGS .159

INSPIRE ONE ANOTHER 163

TIME TO GO ASHORE. 169

SEEING OPPORTUNITY. 175

WHEN YOU DON'T FIT IN, CHOOSE TO STAND OUT . 183

NEW HORIZONS 189

FIND YOUR WINGS .193

THE MAGIC OF FLIGHT. 195

PHOTOS 199

ABOUT THE AUTHOR 211

ACKNOWLEDGMENTS 213

SERVICES 217

WHY I TELL MY STORY

I know what it's like to walk into a room where I seemingly don't fit in—where my presence is immediately noticed, my credentials are questioned, and I'm assumed to be less qualified based on my gender. In addition to being among the first women to graduate from the United States Naval Academy, I was one of the few women, if not the only woman, at each step of my journey as a career naval officer, aviator, and ultimately Navy captain. I know how it feels to be asked time and again to justify my presence and to defend why I had "taken a spot from a more qualified male" (never based on fact, only assumption).

Perhaps that is why I noticed Melanie immediately as she walked into our STEM Summer Institute—a two-week camp dedicated to educating the next generation of young women in STEM, or science, technology, engineering, and mathematics. Melanie sat down a bit removed from the other girls as if she might have felt that she didn't fit in. She was from a different high school than all the others, so she didn't have someone she recognized to sit with. I saw that her head was down and knew I needed to speak with her right away to help her feel included.

Introducing myself, I told Melanie a little about flying, and I saw her face light up. As we connected, I immediately detected an intelligence and spark that I've always loved seeing in young women. "Wow, this girl has a lot going on inside her," I thought.

"I want to be an astronaut," she said. "I like building things, and how cool would it be to build things in space?"

"I too wanted to be an astronaut," I shared. "In fact, several of my friends are astronauts. But it didn't work out for me."

I went on to explain that during my career in the Navy, I had applied to be an astronaut but then found out that I had been medically disqualified for something that seemed incredibly silly to me. At my annual flight physical, my tuberculosis (TB) test indicated positive. Although I did not have TB, I apparently had been exposed. The test indicated that I had a slightly increased chance of contracting the disease.

Under a doctor's supervision, I followed the appropriate six-month regime, which consisted of taking medication in hopes of reducing my chances of contracting TB to a level that was statistically insignificant. Six months of treatment was not sufficient for NASA, however. I was disqualified.

"No fair!" Melanie responded.

"Maybe not," I replied. "Was I disappointed? Yes, but not destroyed. I got to do a lot of cool things."

Our conversation continued throughout the two weeks of camp. I found out that Melanie wanted to become an engineer, and she might become one of the first in her family to go to college. She had come to our camp on scholarship, so I knew she had a financial need and would require help (just as I had) to make her dream come true.

So many thoughts run through my head when I think of Melanie, the young women I continue to work with daily, and even my daughter, Kim Anh. In each of them I see what I saw in myself many years ago: a smart young woman wanting to pursue a path that had not been well traveled before. These young women will face their own challenges as they head out into the world. Some will want to go into STEM careers, where women remain underrepresented (especially in engineering, computer science, and physics) and will need tools to navigate a male-dominated field, much like my own. They will want to push the boundaries of our culture and, each in their own way, will become pioneers.

That is why I tell my story.

I tell my story because of Wardah, the twentysomething woman I met at the "Breaking Barriers: Women in Science" conference sponsored by CRDF Global at the National Press Club. She had been encouraged by my own story in the Navy and is combining her chemical engineering background with a master's degree in international security policy to make the world a better place. She believes, as I do, that more female voices are needed at the global security decision-making table.

Today, women are leading countries, winning more seats in Congress, and leading Fortune 50 companies, yet negative (and unfounded) attitudes toward women in the workplace still prevail. Not long ago while I was at the National Coalition of Girls Schools conference listening to a Women in STEM panel, one woman commented on how someone had recently said to her, "You got the job just because you are a Black woman."

She responded, "I got the job because I am an MIT graduate with a degree in aerospace engineering!"

Despite the impact of the women's movement in the late sixties and the significant progress women have made, this type of behavior still happens today. I don't believe that most men are intentionally biased against women, but I do believe there are too many who think they have the right to make unwanted commentary surrounding the abilities of women.

In education, we speak of "microaggressions," or the indirect, subtle, or unintentional messages directed toward people of a certain race, gender, or culture. And then there are the "macroaggressions," or the overt aggressions, that exist as well. These aggressions, small or large, need to be called out on the spot. They must be stopped if we are to move forward to a more inclusive society. My hope is that by sharing my experiences, I can call attention to and stop these aggressions. The young woman from MIT responded exceptionally well. She diverted the aggression with her shield—her qualifications. Brava!

I also tell my story because of men who still need to understand what it's like to be a minority in the working world. Working as a consultant in an aerospace company just a few years ago, I was completely mystified and infuriated when a man named Curt felt compelled to tell me that his New Year's resolution was to make my work life as difficult as possible.

Finally, I tell my story because of Adelaide, a tiny fifth grader who emits the enthusiasm of a giant. She has the potential to fill up a room, although she is the smallest girl in her entire fifth grade class. I was thrilled to speak her science class, which was filled with wiggly, curious girls, exploring the earth's atmosphere as well as the atmospheres on other planets. Their assignment: Make an alien and its space gear to survive in the environment of their designated planet. Their savvy science teacher asked if I might bring my flight gear to class to talk about what I wore in my high-speed and high-altitude environment. "It might give them some ideas," she said with a wink.

In a fun way, we built a "new pilot." The teacher and I selected one girl at a time to put on a piece of flight equipment—each girl had an opportunity to sample my flight suit, flight boots, helmet, oxygen mask, or flight gloves. I pointed out that each piece was designed with science and technology in mind to keep our aviators safe. As I shared each piece of gear, the girls' energy exploded like a bag of popcorn kernels in the microwave.

Popping up and down, Adelaide burst out, "Did you have a call sign?"

Call signs are nicknames given to all aviators based on certain characteristics an aviator possesses, a twist on someone's name, or a connection to some mistake one might make during training (e.g., *Broadway* for my friend from Manhattan, *Stick* for my friend who is very thin, or *Crash* for the guy who, you guessed it, crashed an airplane).

"Yes, I did!" I exclaimed, my smile broadening across my face. "My call sign was Tinker, as in Tinker Bell. And I had a friend who was quite small, and her call sign was Dot!"

"I'm Dot; I'm Dot," Adelaide exclaimed, still hopping up and down. "Was it like *Top Gun*?"

"Yes, it was!" I said, unexpectedly finding myself hopping up and down as well, her enthusiasm contagious.

Then, to my great surprise, "Dot" (formerly known as Adelaide) burst out singing "Danger Zone," Kenny Loggins's feature song from the movie *Top Gun*.

Hearing the refrain took me back to the eighties, while Dot grounded me in the present. It reminded me that women in traditionally male-dominated careers are not going away. There is still a lot of pioneering for women to do in the world—even in industries where they have historically flourished.

The good news is we don't have to do our work alone. As women, we can support each other—share our stories and the tools we have developed to navigate new frontiers. We are all in this together. We stand on the shoulders of those who have gone before us. I stand on the shoulders of the women who went before me. Now, my shoulders are strong and steady—tested by my experiences—and ready to carry the women who will follow me. That's why I tell my story.

> **AS WOMEN, WE CAN SUPPORT EACH OTHER— SHARE OUR STORIES AND THE TOOLS WE HAVE DEVELOPED TO NAVIGATE NEW FRONTIERS.**

In all of my life experiences, I have served as a pioneer.

Years ago, if you did not know my first name, you might imagine a man, most likely White, standing straight, proud, and tall, wearing the uniform of a naval midshipman and then later a naval officer. That was prior to 1976, when women did not have access to the Academy or most roles within the Naval Service, and their opportunity to serve as democratic citizens in the military was severely limited. But now that image has been shattered, and I am part of the initial cadre of women who did the shattering.

We call ourselves the First Five—the women of the first five classes at the Naval Academy. We are responsible for starting the integration of women into the Academy, ultimately changing its culture and the course of naval history. A seismic shift happened in 1976 as women entered the Naval Academy. Now, after more than forty-five years, women have risen to the ranks of three-star general in the Marine Corps and four-star admiral in the Navy and have even served in combat (something that was prohibited by law until the nineties).

My story and my perspective are unique, and I have lots of things I want to share. Not in the sense of telling you what to do. You'll have to make those decisions for yourself, but I hope my experiences—the good, the bad, and the ugly—will help shape your decisions. The lessons I learned on my journey to survive and thrive in a flying career may guide you along your own path.

While, literally, I learned to fly, metaphorically I did as well. I want to help you fly, too. I'll share some questions to help you find your own wings—to get you thinking about where you are now and where you want to go in the future. My hope is that these thought starters will assist you with identifying your goals and dreams, helping you chart a course to achieve them.

I wish I could tell you that the flight path will be straight and easy, free from any diversions. But that's simply not true. There will be turbulence and some unexpected challenges along the way. Although times have changed, they have not changed enough. There will still be many out there who will tell you that because you are a woman, and perhaps a woman of color as well, that your dreams are too big. You will be told in both subtle and not-so-subtle ways that you do not belong.

Don't believe them! I know your future is bright, and it belongs to you. You can learn to soar! They are wrong, and I am living proof that they are wrong. And you will be too. That is why I tell my story.

PART ONE:
GRITTING IT OUT

Some of us have great runways already built for us.
If you have one, take off. But if you don't have one, realize
it is your responsibility to grab a shovel and build one
for yourself and for those who will follow after you.

—AMELIA EARHART

DREAMS OF FLYING

So where should I begin my story? I guess I should start where most stories start. At the beginning.

Actually, my story begins before I was born. Biologically, I come from a long line that consists mostly of intelligent women, teachers, and nurses. They were the smart women in their high schools—graduated as valedictorians or salutatorians—but they did not have the same opportunities that were available to me as I came of age.

Cosmically speaking, I am the daughter of a group of women pioneers, "women of the air" or "fly girls" as they were known. Amelia Earhart and Bessie Coleman opened the way for women pilots in the earliest days of aviation. Then Jackie Cochrane, Nancy Love,

> **I AM THE DAUGHTER OF A GROUP OF WOMEN PIONEERS, "WOMEN OF THE AIR" OR "FLY GIRLS."**

and the Women Airforce Service Pilots (WASP) opened the door for women to fly in the military—a door that slammed closed for several decades after World War II. Then came Captain Rosemary Mariner, Captain Jane O'Dea, Captain M. L. Griffin, and the others who began flying as the Navy opened flight training to women in 1973.

As a fifth grader, I read about Betsy Ross, Juliette Low, Sojourner Truth, Helen Keller, Amelia Earhart, Wilma Rudolph, Louisa May Alcott, Susan B. Anthony, Clara Barton, Marie Curie, and Harriett Tubman. Little did I know their stories would ultimately influence my life in a dramatic way.

For me it began as a child in the sixties. On warm summer days in my backyard, I would lie on my back in the grass, examining cloud formations against the clear blue sky. I watched airplanes, but I had no context, no role models to consult about my feelings on flying. Back in the sixties, when the idea of flying became a dream of mine, there were few female pilots.

Asleep at night in the comfort of my room, I had dreams of flying without an aircraft. With arms outstretched, I would soar over the contours of the rolling hills below, feeling the wind in my face as I flew. Over and over again, as a child and into my adolescent years, I would drift into those dreams at night, sometimes flying high, sometimes low over the peaks and dips of the hillsides. Still today, whenever I see rolling hills like the ones that surround my home in Nashville, I am immediately brought back to those dreams.

Then, I had no idea where my dreams might lead. Today, I *know* where they did.

POSSIBILITIES

"**Y**ou are going to college," my parents told their three children.

There was no other option—Dan, Jim, and I were all going to college. Due to limited family finances, our parents were not able to pay for college, so they challenged us to find our own way to accomplish this. But the looming question in our young heads was, "How in the world are we going to do that?"

All three of us were smart and had learned how to be self-reliant as a result of facing challenging financial times at home. Although we had part-time jobs at various points in our teen years, my mother reminded us that school was our job—*our primary job*. We were expected to go to college, which meant that studying hard and getting good grades took precedence over making money. We were given high expectations with no excuses.

Today, as an educator, I am struck by how profound that message and challenge was to me and my brothers. Sadly, I see students opt out of going to college as early as eighth grade because they don't believe they can go. My brothers and I were taught early on to believe that college was in our reach. Many young people are not so lucky. One of the reasons I am in education today is to encourage, challenge, and introduce our young people to the idea that going to college is an option within their reach regardless of their background, socioeconomic status, or any other discriminator. I can help them find a way.

With the help of others, the three of us found a way. My older brother, Dan, two years my senior, was encouraged by his football coach to apply to the Air Force Academy, kicking off our family's military careers. Jim, two and a half years my junior, would later attend the Air Force Academy as well. Well beyond anything our family could afford, the Air Force Academy provided an elite education.

In high school, I became aware that I longed for more—not more things or more money, but more experiences, more adventure. I wanted more out of life, and I wanted to do something different. My small town in Michigan, as beautiful as it was, did not offer enough to hold me. I fully remember when we visited Dan for Parents' Weekend in Colorado Springs in September of 1977. As I took in the grandeur of the Air Force Academy (the Cadet Area is a national historic landmark) against the background of the Rocky Mountains, visited his classes, and walked the grounds of the campus, I knew deep inside myself that I would never be satisfied with an education anything less than what he was experiencing.

I began researching how I might find my way to such an education. Whenever I received a letter of interest from a college, I would fill out the "for more information" card and send it in. As more and more college information arrived in the mail, I stuffed several brown paper grocery bags with educational "possibilities" and pored over them in my room at night. Those grocery bags represented unlimited possibilities for my future. The contents inside exposed me to ideas and parts of the country never before imagined. I looked at Harvard, Wellesley, and Rensselaer Polytechnic Institute as well as many others. Captivated by the world beyond our small town, I still wondered, "How will I be able to afford this?" I had the grades, the intellect, and the ability, but not the money.

With my brother at the Air Force Academy, I began investigating the different service academies. Following on the heels of the women's movement of the late sixties, changes in higher education now allowed elite institutions to be open to women. Ivy League colleges such as Yale, Princeton, and Harvard became fully coeducational. Military academies also began opening their doors to women—but only because they were directed by law to accommodate women. On October 7, 1975, President Ford signed Public Law 94-106, authorizing women to be admitted into the service academies.[1]

I discovered that the service academies would give me the elite education I desired as well as a full-ride scholarship. West Point did not appeal to me, and going to the Air Force Academy meant I would be Dan's little sister again. I was determined to strike out on my own. The Naval Academy in Annapolis, Maryland, captured my attention. Often considered the elite, the Naval Academy is the primary commissioning source for Navy and Marine Corps officers. Those who enter the institution and graduate join a long tradition of distinguished officers. They are promoted more often and to higher ranks within the Naval Service. Yes, the US Naval Academy was where I wanted to go.

After I told my family, my mother pulled out her typewriter, and we began the admissions process. My brother, still at the Air Force

---

1   94th Congress, first session, 1975.

Academy, responded in anger, "How could you be so stupid to want to go to a place like that?" Dan was a member of the class of 1981, which included the second class of women allowed at the Air Force Academy. He had witnessed firsthand how poorly women were being treated at the service academies, from the unrelenting scrutiny to the overt harassment. By calling me "stupid," he thought I might look elsewhere.

Undeterred, I recognized the incredible opportunity to get the education I desperately wanted but my family could not afford. The long, arduous application process began in earnest during the spring of my junior year. The process was the same for both women and men, although admission of women was restricted. The target number for admission of the first class of women at the Naval Academy (Class of 1980) was eighty, and for the next eight years the goal gradually increased to approximately one hundred women.

Application to the service academies is a two-part process: through the Academy and through the political offices that nominate candidates to the school. After completing my application to the Academy, I wrote letters to my two state senators and the congressman from my district expressing my desire to be nominated for a position of appointment to the Academy.

After initial review of my application by the Academy, I was required to take a physical exam and perform a physical fitness test to determine whether I was physically and medically qualified to become a midshipman. (Students at the Naval Academy are called "midshipmen," while students at the Air Force Academy and West Point are called "cadets.") Being both a runner and a swimmer and having no issues with my physical health, I easily qualified both medically and physically.

Then, the interview process started. I was interviewed by a local Academy representative. Known as a Blue and Gold Officer, this is a volunteer who helps guide prospective candidates through the admission process. From there, interview panels were set up by my senators and congressman. They asked the standard questions they asked all male candidates. Then came the question, "As a woman why do you think you can make it through the Academy?"

The question felt unfair. But then, all the interviewers were male, so of course they asked. I was the elephant in the room—a woman, not your typical candidate. Perhaps they were trying to push my buttons or see how much grit I had for the challenge ahead. It felt like they were really asking, "Why does a nice girl like you want to go to a place like this?" Looking back, it might have been my very first encounter with sexism.

Unfazed, I responded, "Well, I grew up with two brothers, one younger and one older, and I've always been able to do everything they can do. I've worked harder and have better grades than my older brother, who is at the Air Force Academy. I know what I am getting myself into."

Or so I thought.

By Christmas, both senators and my congressman gave me nominations to the Naval Academy, which increased my odds that I would be given an appointment. About two out of ten students given nominations to the Academy receive appointments, so with three nominations, my chances were good.

In February of my senior year, I received an offer of appointment to the US Naval Academy. Although I was excited, I was equally hesitant. Despite the confidence I had shown in my interview, I wondered, "What kind of woman goes to an academy? Was I tough enough? Was I smart enough?"

I remember walking the halls of my high school looking around at the other young women, assessing their academic and athletic abilities. Were they more qualified? No. I was as smart and athletic as any woman I knew. Students at my high school, and even my guidance counselor, didn't understand why I was considering this path. Many thought I was enlisting in the Navy, on my way to chip paint off hulls of ships. "But you are so smart; why are you joining the Navy?" someone asked.

They did not understand what the Naval Academy offered. They had no idea I had been awarded a full-ride scholarship to an elite university. But I knew. The Naval Academy was my opportunity to change my life.

My mother prodded me to make a decision. Seeing the challenges women were facing at the Air Force Academy, my brother told me not to do it. While I appreciated his brotherly concern, I would make my own decision. I looked deep inside myself. I truly believed I had everything I needed to succeed. It took me over a month, but I accepted my appointment.

THE NAVAL ACADEMY WAS MY OPPORTUNITY TO CHANGE MY LIFE.

After making this major decision, I never looked back, and I have never regretted my choice. Even today, I give thoughtful and careful consideration to every major decision I make in my life, and I always stick with it. When facing a major choice in your life, take time to do your research and gather all the information you can. Then search within yourself. What are your dreams, desires, and motivations? Then, and only then, make your decision. Once it's made, you don't need to second-guess it. Be perceptive when examining possibilities and settle into the fact that with each new possibility there will be decisions to make and actions to take. Look forward and move on.

PLEBE SUMMER

O n an airplane by myself for the first time in my life, I prepared to depart from my hometown. I looked out the window as the plane rolled down the runway, tears streaming down my face. I was leaving my family and everything familiar, taking off for the unknown. Final destination: Annapolis, Maryland.

The very next day was Induction Day, the day that would change my life forever. On July 6, 1979, in the steamy, nearly liquid, heat of Annapolis, I anxiously raised my right hand, took the Oath of a Midshipman, and became a member of the fourth class of women to enter the US Naval Academy.

IN THAT FIERCELY INTENSE MOMENT, I KNEW THE CHALLENGE OF A LIFETIME HAD BEGUN.

In that fiercely intense moment, I knew the challenge of a lifetime had begun.

That day, plebe summer began in earnest.[2] Designed to turn civilians into midshipmen, plebe summer is a hellish, six-week training program required of all incoming freshmen of the Naval Academy.

When you enter the Naval Academy, they strip from you everything that is familiar. They take away your civilian clothes and give you a uniform. They cut your hair. They tell you when to get up, when to eat, when to go to bed—breaking you down as an individual, then building you up as a team. They are developing midshipmen one day at a time. In the military, it is critical that you work as a team. Lives depend on it, particularly in combat. The process is referred to as resocialization. What you previously held to be true, that the individual matters most, is transformed to a new set of values, beliefs, and norms—that the unit or team matters the most.

You even learn a new language—the endless acronyms and the formulaic responses expected in the military. I can still remember my five basic plebe responses: 1) Yes, sir; 2) No, sir; 3) Aye, aye, sir (meaning you comprehend the order and will take action); 4) I'll find out, sir; and 5) No excuse, sir. During plebe summer and into most of our plebe year, unless asked a detailed question, these were the only responses we were allowed to give.

A similar experience happens in boot camp or officer candidate school. But at the Naval Academy and at the other service academies, the drilling goes on for four years. Four long years. It all starts with the six weeks of plebe summer.

This approach may seem harsh, but it serves a crucial purpose given the military's mission. When we are in the midst of life's chal-

---

2   A "plebe" is a first-year midshipman. In historical terms, plebe refers to the lower class or lowest class of citizens.

lenges, we may not always see or understand the larger purpose of what we are experiencing. But it is important to remember that it will serve us for the rest of our lives. My experience at the Naval Academy, and certainly plebe summer, changed me forever.

A significant portion of plebe summer is physical conditioning. We marched, we ran, we did endless pushups and squats. And of course, we took placement tests and registered for classes for the upcoming academic year.

The physical challenges were not the hard part, at least not for me; the mental and emotional challenges were far more difficult. Daily we had to memorize "plebe rates"—the written and unwritten rules of the Navy—and learn the chain of command. We also had to memorize daily menus and articles from the *Washington Post*. Not only did we have to learn new requirements each day, but we had to remember each previous day's requirements and be ready to be tested at a moment's notice.

"What are the *Laws of the Navy*, Miss Bell?" "What is the menu for lunch, Miss Bell?" "Who are the officers of the watch today, Miss Bell?" "What is the mission of the Naval Service, Miss Bell?" Our squad leaders asked again and again, pushing us deeper and deeper into our memory banks until we could not find an answer. Then they would rage all over us for not knowing the answer. They tried over and over to break us down, and sometimes they did. But we learned to pick ourselves up again and again.

Millie, my Naval Academy roommate, recently showed me a letter she had written to her mother during plebe summer. She told her how I was getting unwanted attention from an upperclassman and how my squad leader was not letting me eat. As she read the letter, I was thrown back into my plebe year. The early-morning wake-ups, the physical training, the mental gymnastics, the harassment, and the stifling Annapolis heat. To this day, when I smell starched cotton like the white sailor uniforms we wore as plebes, beads of sweat form on the back of my neck.

I don't remember too much about the unwanted attention from the upperclassman, but I do remember not eating. One of my squad leaders thought it was quite fun to mess with his plebes at each meal, requiring us to sing for our meals and asking unrelenting questions on our plebe rates. Only after he was satisfied that we had sung enough songs and answered enough questions would he allow us to eat. Of course, by then the mealtime was over, and we were dismissed. (I now find it incredible that this squad leader was not stripped of his duties for not letting us eat. Today I doubt that this would happen, as I believe there is more oversight. At least, I hope that is the case.)

I'd run back to Millie's room (the only time we did not room together was plebe summer) and grab anything I could from her "chow package" (the treats she received from home). Angry and hungry—but never crying—I would throw a handful of food into my mouth and head onto the next event. We quickly learned to compartmentalize our emotions, only allowing them out when we deemed it safe.

Interestingly, our male plebe classmates treated us well. That is, until plebe summer ended and the Brigade of Midshipmen, the entire student body, returned for the academic year. Then we were pushed to the side. Suddenly, the male plebes did not want to hang out with us. One clear reason stands out. Our dorms were coed, although if you take into consideration that women represented only a small percentage of the student body, the dorms were more all-male with a light sprinkling of women. The men's rooms had black name tags on the doors, while the women's rooms had white name tags, making it quite easy to single out where we lived.

For our first two years, the regulations required that we leave our doors open whenever a man was in a woman's room or vice versa. The open door, meant to protect us, became an invitation for any upperclassman to come in at any time to harass everyone in the room. "Just to see what was going on," they would say. Our male classmates did not want us in their rooms, nor did they want to be in ours. Associating with women only made their lives harder.

The Academy—and particularly plebe summer—is a struggle for everyone, but especially so for women in those early years. As the fall term started, we felt isolated physically, mentally, and emotionally, like small islands in the midst of a vast ocean of men. Not only did we feel isolated; we *were* isolated. It was a harbinger of many more challenges to come.

DEFENDING OUR PRESENCE

P lebe year continued at an exhausting pace. The running, the questioning, the yelling, the memorization never stopped. On top of academics and adjusting to college life in general, we had the ongoing challenges as plebes at the bottom of the hierarchical pile. It all rolls downhill as they say, and at the bottom are the plebes, catching it all.

Although all of us were plebes, as women, we stood out—all the time. We had to put up with the same challenges (physical, mental, emotional) the men experienced, and then more. Far more. We had the vexing challenge of plowing hardscrabble ground that had never been touched before—at that time, it had been over 130 years of tradition as a male-only military school. As women began entering the Academy in 1976, we represented a small percentage of each incoming class. In my class of 1983, the fourth class of women to enter the Academy, women represented only 6 percent of the overall freshman class. Today, women represent nearly 30 percent of the student body.

Although the law said we could be there, the attitudes and actions of others told us differently. Two significant events occurred during my plebe year, both of which will be forever remembered by every woman there at the time.

The first was a visit by the Chief of Naval Operations (CNO), the most senior officer in the United States Navy. The CNO came to speak to the entire Brigade of Midshipmen as part of a regular lecture series. As the CNO concluded his remarks, he opened the floor to questions. One extremely brave woman, Kathy Bustle from the class of 1982, asked the admiral something to this effect: "Sir, you have opened the Naval Academy to women; therefore, why has the Navy not opened more jobs to women?" Or as Millie remembered it, Kathy said, "Many of the women of the Class of 1980 will receive desk jobs. Why have us train here if we cannot go into combat?" At that time, the combat exclusion laws were in effect, which did not allow women to fly combat aircraft or serve on combatant ships.

The admiral's response was to turn the question around on this brave young woman. He responded along the lines of, "So are you telling me that women do not belong here?"

The audience's response is burned into my memory forever. We women watched in complete shock as over four thousand men of the Brigade of Midshipmen (our classmates, friends, and upperclassmen) rose to their feet clapping vehemently, giving the CNO a standing ovation. The sound of that thunderous clapping vibrates in my head as I remember that evening. The most senior officer in the Navy had questioned our presence at the Academy.

Deflated, we women departed the field house with our heads hung low. The smell of male superiority hung in the air. Our male classmates carried on their conversations but avoided looking in our direction. We said nothing but later discussed the event privately in our rooms. "How can the most senior officer in the Navy question our presence?" we asked each other. We did not have answers, but we knew we were in this together.

As if to pour salt in our wounds, a short time later, an article by James Webb was published in the *Washingtonian* magazine. Titled "Women Can't Fight," it was an incendiary commentary about women at the Naval Academy.[3] Webb, a revered war hero, author, and Marine, clearly opposed the presence of women at the Academy. In his opinion, our presence softened the Naval Academy and also our military. I choose not to get into more specifics on Webb's article as it might only incite more controversy. Suffice it to say, the negative effects lasted for decades.

More destructively for us as individuals, his article fanned the flame of resentment toward us and gave the men the perceived authority to treat women poorly, as less than, rather than as equals. The women were challenged by our male classmates and upperclassmen to defend not only ourselves but also our collective presence as women at the Naval Academy.

Our upperclassmen constantly pitted us against our male classmates and one another. Heartless, yes, but the experiences helped us to build our grit, determination, and resistance, skills that our future careers would eventually demand. My roommate was forced to debate Webb's article at the dinner tables and take the position that women should not be at the Naval Academy. I was luckier. I was required to take the position that women should be at the Academy, while my male plebe classmates were told to take the position that women did not belong.

---

3   James Webb, "Women Can't Fight," *Washingtonian*, November 1, 1979, https://www.washingtonian.com/1979/11/01/jim-webb-women-cant-fight/.

The challenges extended into the academic environment, where military instructors called us out as well. I remember getting an A on a chemistry exam. The officer who was my professor handed it back to me with a snarky, "Don't rest on your laurels, Miss Bell." I believe I got the only A on that exam, and instead of praising me, he did the opposite. I would find out years later that another male professor intentionally failed women in his classes. It wasn't until these women had to take summer school that his antics were realized by the administration. Defending ourselves was not an easy task. We had very little power, especially as first-year midshipmen.

The constant need to defend our presence was both exhausting and crushing.

"Why am I doing this?"

I asked myself that question many times at the Naval Academy and especially in the early years. Getting a college degree at any other university would have been much easier. I had to constantly remind myself that I was engaging in something far bigger than myself and far more important than obtaining a college degree. We were opening doors and building a runway for ourselves and for the women who would follow us.

During the weeks following the CNO's comments and the publication of the Webb article, there were few words we could utter, other than the fact that the law allowed us to be there. The men considered our presence an experiment, one that could be proven wrong. Yes, we were demoralized, but

YES, WE WERE DEMORALIZED, BUT WE WERE NOT LEAVING. THE LAW OPENED THE DOOR, AND WE WERE DETERMINED TO KEEP IT OPEN.

we were not leaving. The law opened the door, and we were determined to keep it open.

What we came to realize was that our actions (over many years), not our words, would show that we belonged at the Naval Academy and in the Naval Service. Standing on the shoulders of the women who rebelled in the sixties, we were there to get an education accessible nowhere else and open a new pathway for women to become new types of Navy and Marine Corps officers. Our ongoing presence day after day, year after year, would change attitudes toward women and, ultimately, validate the law.

SISTERS, WE THREE

Each person who goes through a service academy is changed forever.

The Academy is not for everyone—man or woman. First, you must want to be there for yourself, not for your parents and not for continuing the family legacy of Naval Service. The highly structured life, along with the mental, physical, and emotional discipline required, can be too much for young adults.

One does not go through challenges like the Naval Academy alone. At least one shouldn't. When going through extreme challenges in our lives, we need to find others to sustain us.

> **WHEN GOING THROUGH EXTREME CHALLENGES IN OUR LIVES, WE NEED TO FIND OTHERS TO SUSTAIN US.**

During my time at the Academy, my two roommates, Millie and Karen, were my primary life support. Living in one small dorm room with each other for four years, we were a constant source of encouragement for one another.

The only time the three of us did not live together was during plebe summer. At the beginning of the summer, we started with five women in our company.[4] One left that summer. Another departed during our sophomore or "youngster" year. Karen, Millie, and I stuck together all four years, and to this day, we remain closely connected. Millie, the fiery redhead from the far reaches of northern Michigan; Karen, the stalwart, spunky brunette from Rhode Island; and me, the tall, curly-haired one, also from Michigan.

Each of us were from humble beginnings, as were the majority of my classmates. What connected us early on was our burning desire for an education that was beyond the means of our families, the opportunity to serve our country, and the willingness to be change agents. Millie, Karen, and I were smart, motivated, and undeterred. We were going to help one another make it through the Academy. We found an indomitable strength within ourselves and collectively with each other.

In our room we shared a sink, a shower, and closet space. We also shared the daily struggles of our lives. We laughed, we screamed, but we barely cried, as tears were unacceptable in that place. "We were so geared up to be strong. We feared being perceived as weak," Millie recently shared. "During the tough times, it was hard to reach out to anyone without the fear of feeling like a failure or that you were the only one struggling."

---

4   At that time, the Brigade of Midshipmen was divided into six battalions with six companies per battalion. Each company held about 120 midshipmen.

We routinely stuffed our emotions deep down inside ourselves, and only began to unpack our experiences years later.

Millie, Karen, and I often spoke about how we felt as if we lived in a fishbowl, always under constant scrutiny, except when we were in the solace of our room. To say we know one another well is an understatement. Sisters, we three. While I do not have a biological sister, the bond among the three of us is real and will endure for the rest of our lives. Struggle will do that. You do not go through the challenges we did as women in a distinct minority to our male classmates without bonding and bonding deeply.

It is hard to process all that happened at the Naval Academy. Four years of grueling challenge and incredible personal growth, punctuated by experiences of profound joy knowing that I, along with my women classmates, was making history. I stayed because I liked challenges, I wanted the elite education the Academy offered, and I knew I was part of something much bigger than myself.

The bond one builds with the Academy is strong and filled with complexities and complications. It is a love/hate relationship, and many of us women graduates have it. My friend Christy often reminds me of a comment I once made about the Naval Academy: "Oh yes, Annapolis, the beautiful place where I was imprisoned for four years."

Maybe that comment was a bit harsh, a bit cynical, but I have felt that way on many occasions. I do, however, remember that I volunteered to be there. No one forced me. On one hand, the Naval Academy provided a springboard to a different life—one of challenge, education, international travel, and the opportunity to serve my country as a naval officer.

On the other hand, my experience came at a cost. Many of us women have emotional scars from our experience. When you are told again and again that you do not belong, that you are not qualified, and that you are not valued as a person, your self-esteem wanes. We arrived as the best and brightest women our nation had to offer. By the time we graduated, we doubted ourselves. We felt tarnished, beaten down in fact.

Attrition was high for us women—just over 40 percent. Ninety women entered the Academy in my class of 1983. Only fifty-three graduated and went on to careers as Navy and Marine Corps officers. I'll not claim to know all the reasons why women left, as each are quite personal. Some likely left because of academics, a few because of physical challenges. I do believe that some left because of the unrelenting challenge of not fitting in. They threw up their hands and said, "I've had enough" and chose to go to school elsewhere.

If you leave the Academy, you may be viewed as a quitter—as supported by the ethos of the Academy. You don't transfer. You quit. I can only imagine the shame that might be attached to a decision to leave and how bad it must have been for those women, to be willing to endure the shame of "quitting" and choose to leave anyway. Years later, I would learn why some of the women left. Their stories are hard, and they are not mine to tell. But they underscore the essential need for all of us to share our stories if we are going to continue to move the needle of change. (This is why I chose to write this book.)

Returning to the Academy, as you can imagine, is fraught with emotions. "I feel like Superwoman in my work as a banker, but going back to Annapolis is my kryptonite," Millie said to me many years ago. Today that is no longer true. Millie, Karen, and I, the three sisters, return for nearly every five-year reunion. Returning to the Academy has been part of our healing process.

I have three favorite pictures of the three of us from our time at the Academy. One is of us standing together in our dress drill uniforms. Smiles across our faces, we are wearing our starched white pants, black wool jackets, belts, and white gloves and holding our rifles at our sides. We are standing shoulder to shoulder before our last parade, proud and filled with anticipation of our upcoming graduation, looking as if we are ready to take on the world. Because it was our last parade, we would never wear those uniforms again.

The other two photos are from after the parade. In one, we are wet from having jumped into the fountain, a longtime tradition. We are laughing joyfully, wearing the T-shirts from our favorite deli, Chick and Ruth's. The final photo is the same shot but from the back. What captures me first are the broad shoulders we have and then the fun messages emblazoned on our backs: Naughty, Nasty, and Nice. Millie wore "Naughty," Karen wore "Nasty," and I wore "Nice." That picture is a nod to our personalities, while showing the love we had for each other and the fun we shared through the years. The pictures serve as a good reminder that our experience was not all about struggle; we had quite a lot of fun too.

Millie and Karen continue to sustain me nearly forty years later. At one of our annual gatherings, Karen gave Millie and me the same pin to wear on our jackets. She also kept one for herself. The metal pin holds the silhouettes of three women—connected shoulder to shoulder, hip to hip, each with a heart at the center. The pin holds great symbolism for us. It represents who we were, who we are now, and how we will always be connected.

BUILDING OUR RESISTANCE

Finally, after nearly eleven months, our plebe year ended, and we became upperclassmen, which gave us a bit more freedom. Occasionally we got a weekend off and could get away from the Academy, a welcome respite. Some of the harassment stopped for our male peers, but not for the women. In fact, the negative comments and actions toward women continued throughout our four years at the Academy. At times it felt relentless.

Our upperclassmen tried again and again to make the point that we did not belong. Comments about women would be tossed into the air like confetti when we were in earshot. "She only got here because she is a woman." "Did you see what that woman was doing?" "Who does she think she is?"

Some aimed their verbal attacks at us directly, such as, "Why did you take a spot from a man?" More often, they were comments about some "other" woman. The men wanted us to claim responsibility for these "other" women and get us to agree that one specific woman did not belong. Therefore, the subtext of their attack was that all women did not belong. They were trying to divide and conquer.

The comments stung, particularly because the women who came to the Naval Academy were the best and brightest our country had to offer. We were valedictorians, varsity athletes, and student leaders. Sometimes we lost sight of our talents and abilities and allowed ourselves to be momentarily dragged down. Yet we persisted. Eventually, over the many days and months, we became immune to the provocations. They fell onto our shoulders, and we brushed them away. "Oh, just another day at the Academy."

I can clearly remember a conversation with a male classmate named Curt one evening at our company dinner tables. (I now see the relationship between our "company" tables at the Naval Academy and "company" tables in the private sector. How often are the tables in company boardrooms inhospitable to women? Still too often, I imagine.)

I was a sophomore, or "youngster" in Academy terms, and he was a junior, or second classman. We were having yet another conversation about women at the Academy. "Will this ever stop?" I wondered in my head, while grinding my teeth.

Pointing several tables away, he said, "Now she is overweight and cannot run the mile. You've got to agree, Barb, that she does not belong here."

I felt the anger rising in me, almost transitioning to fury. "She" was not my responsibility, as she was not in my chain of command. Then I saw my opportunity. I was a runner, and he was not. "I don't know whether she can run the mile or not, but if you want to meet me tomorrow at 6:00 a.m., I'd be happy to go for a run with you."

He sheepishly backed away from our conversation, never to bother me again. I had stood my ground. He got my point: I was responsible for myself, not all women.

While most of the harassment was verbal, there was overt bullying. We had one classmate, I'll call him "Richard," who seemed to make it his personal mission to bully women. In particular, he bullied my roommate Millie. My stomach still turns as I remember Millie's experience with him. They had a class together, and from the moment she would walk into class, Richard would start needling her. Fairly benign in the beginning, what one might call microaggressions today, the comments escalated during the semester into direct insults. No one intervened—not the other men, not even the professor.

One day Richard threw something at Millie, just missing her eye. She had had enough. She grabbed him by his collar, placing her face in his and raged, "I don't give a f#@% what you say, but don't *ever* touch me, throw something at me, or hit me ever again!"

Only then did he leave her alone. Looking back, Millie is not sure what hurt her more, Richard's actions or the fact that no one intervened on her behalf.

Richard is the same classmate who, during our mandatory mile swim, grabbed me and pulled me underwater, attempting to swim over me. When I bobbed back to the surface, he glanced back at me with a crass smile on his face. Luckily, I was a good swimmer. I dove underwater, grabbed his ankles, pulled him back with all my might and swam over him. Fully enraged, I increased my speed to ensure I beat him to the finish line.

Karen shared with me years later that some of the male instructors at surface warfare school liked to select the woman or women in the class as examples and would "mess" with them within the confines of the class to see if they could fluster them. "The best thing to do was to approach the situation professionally, use your training, stay level headed, and do the best job possible without trying to attract any extra attention," Karen explained. "Just doing the things you would normally do to be the best example and represent your command well generally applied in all situations."

There were so many more incidents like these, but individually they seem less important today. What is important is what we took away from those experiences, how they made us stronger.

WHAT IS IMPORTANT IS WHAT WE TOOK AWAY FROM THOSE EXPERIENCES, HOW THEY MADE US STRONGER.

I have no idea how my career would have been different if I had gone into the corporate world instead. I bet I would have welcomed those challenges as well. But I wonder who I would be without the crucible of learning that was the Naval Academy. As poet Robert Frost said, "I took the road less traveled by and that has made all the difference."

I realize today that not much gets me riled up as a result of my experiences at the Naval Academy. But I do engage when it is critical to do so. Words hurt, but you have to examine the source and context. Sometimes hurtful comments are only confetti. When they are, just brush them off and let them flutter away. Other times, they are boulders intended to trip you up and cause you to fall. That is when it is time to engage and take action. Stand up, "get big," as I like to say (like Millie did), and let them know in no uncertain terms that the behavior stops now. Don't let them pull you under. Pick up some speed and "outswim" them.

The adversities I faced also taught me grit and determination. Some people mistakenly think that these two qualities are something we are born with. I am here to tell you that they are skills that can be built. Grit is built one challenge at a time. We push forward, make mistakes, fall down, pick ourselves up, dust ourselves off, and take the next step forward.

If you can build these skills of grit and determination, they will serve you well for the rest of your life. Challenge yourself, volunteer for difficult assignments, lead a new project, and lean into adversity. Take risks and be willing to fail. As Albert Einstein said, "Failure is success in progress."

If you want to know what grit and determination look like, see the picture of the fifty-three women of the United States Naval Academy Class of 1983. If I had pictures of the women in the three classes of 1980, 1981, and 1982 that preceded us and the class of 1984 that followed us ("the First Five"), I would show them as well.

We had an unrelenting commitment to being pioneers. We struggled, we became fighters, we survived, and ultimately, we learned to thrive. We became toughened by our experiences, and sometimes numbed by them. We put one foot in front of the other, day after day. As we say in the military, we "carried on." We were the newest generation of women claiming our rightful place in the military.

LEAN INTO THE HILLS

Although legally we had a right to be at the Academy, we were not wanted. We were only going to survive if we treated our four years at the Naval Academy as a marathon rather than a sprint. My experience as a distance runner, in both cross-country and track, and as a swimmer, helped me tremendously. In cross-country, track, and competitive swimming, you mostly compete against yourself. You seek to improve who you are as an athlete—your form, your times, your mental edge—and then you go out at each competition to improve your personal record in each event.

These sports literally get into your pores. They teach you the importance of grit, determination, and hard work. The emotional, mental, and physical lessons involved in distance running are learned by placing one foot in front of another, again and again and again. To build the miles for the foundation you need, it takes consistency and dedication to daily practice. When you reach the point of exhaustion in a race, you learn to truly test your endurance and run a few more miles, and to push through the pain to achieve your goal.

Although I only swam for a year, I ran for all four years at the Academy. Running with the women's track and cross-country teams was my escape. The women's weight room was our sanctuary—no men allowed. Many days we ran outside the gates of the Academy and through the town of Annapolis. As we exited the gates, the feeling of freedom washed over us. We felt lighter, knowing that at least for the next hour or two, we were not confined by the Academy. We could be young women runners—just like at any other college—laughing, joking, talking about cute guys, and being goofy without being judged. With each mile, we bonded deeply with one another.

Running was also a safe haven where we felt respected by our male cross-country and track teammates. As an added bonus, we could outrun most of the men in the brigade who were not on the team! My friend Virginia, an elite runner from Maryland, says, "We got less crap and more respect because we could do something they could not. Running helped level the playing field." Well, in one area at least.

Our coaches were male Marine Corps aviators. Major Sheedy was the motivator, Major Dunham the drill sergeant. Major Sheedy's approach to running hills was to remind us to keep our heads up, keep our speed up, and lean into the hills. I can still hear his voice as we would approach a steep hill: "I love it; I just love it!" We were coached to never stop at the top of a hill to catch our breath, but instead to use the momentum gained from pressing into the hill to flow through to the other side. *Find your flow* is how I might describe it today.

I smile when I think of Major Dunham and Major Sheedy and the lessons I learned from them. Sometimes, you need your internal drill sergeant, sometimes your internal motivator, and sometimes both. For me, their coaching was filled with good life advice that I still follow. I remind myself that no obstacle is too big to overcome. I lean into challenges with a full, open heart and power up each "hill." Triumphant at the summit, I don't stop, but roll straight into the next adventure.

You can do that too.

Maybe your challenge is that first difficult college calculus class. You want to become an engineer, but summiting calculus is the first hill in your journey. Dig deep, keep your head up, and lean into it. Find a tutor. Practice, practice, practice. Then summit that hill. And keep going. It gets easier on the back side, I promise.

Or perhaps you have an opportunity for a promotion at work. Rely on the foundation you have built and all the professional experience you have gained. Prepare for the conversation. Get a coach or mentor to help. Then put one foot in front of the other, walk into your boss's office, and go ask for the promotion!

I remember asking for a raise when I was a business consultant. I had been working at this company for several months, and I knew they liked my work because it was commented on regularly. Knowing that women have a tendency to not ask for what they want, I decided differently. I began dropping hints to the vice president, sharing that I wanted to discuss a pay increase at my six-month contract review. When the day came, I was prepared. The vice president asked, "So how much do you want?" I gave him the number, which was nearly double my hourly rate at the time. He accepted it right away, making me the highest-paid consultant in the company.

Life is full of "hills." Don't shy away from those steep climbs. Speed up and lean into every challenge. Be persistent. Rise up

DON'T SHY AWAY FROM THOSE STEEP CLIMBS. SPEED UP AND LEAN INTO EVERY CHALLENGE.

every incline you face, so that when that "Oh shit!" hill appears ahead, you are ready to take it on.

FINDING OURSELVES

For the first two years at the Academy, we women struggled to fit in, trying to be like the guys. We wanted to be seen as equals to the men.

Our daily uniforms were similar to theirs: black slacks; black web belt with brass buckle; black men's shirts with our last names embroidered just above the left pocket; and long black men's ties knotted with Windsor knots and tucked in between buttons three and four on our shirts. We wore essentially no makeup (why bother?) and no jewelry except for the regulation brushed gold ball post earrings that essentially served to keep our pierced ears open, might we have the opportunity to wear real earrings sometime in the future. Our hair was cut short, although not as short as the men. Regulations required that our hair be above the top of our collar and not extend much away from our head.

Overall, it was not a highly attractive look, but then again, our physical appearance wasn't our biggest worry at the time. Still, I remember the stinging words of an upperclassman early in my plebe year. "I thought there were five new women; I only see four. Oh, there she is," he said, pointing to me. "She looks like a guy anyway."

Of course, our body shapes and sizes were different than the men, but the only piece of our uniform that marked us as different were our hats, referred to as "covers" in military jargon. So it was always easy to spot a woman. Although we ran with the guys, PT'ed (physical training) with the guys, marched with the guys, went to class with the guys, and lived among the guys, our different hats made us stand out no matter how hard we tried to blend in.

The flip side of our challenge to fit in was our struggle to be women. Granted, we didn't think much about being women the first two years. We were just trying to survive. We had few opportunities to wear civilian clothes (almost none our plebe year). As we became upperclassmen, we could wear civilian "girl clothes" a little more frequently, but only on the weekends. When we did get dressed up, we were criticized as well. I believe it was a shock for the men to see us as women after days and then years of seeing us as WUBAs (Working Uniform Blue Alpha), the derogatory term men sometimes used for us.

We wanted to be equals and also be women. The tension was always there. These were our college years after all, where men and women intermingle and date, but it hardly felt like college. Sometimes in social settings we tried to be women and not midshipmen, but it didn't seem to work. I can remember being at an off-campus party with several midshipmen who did not know that I was one as well. One young man showed interest in me. This is how I remember our conversation:

"So, do you work or go to school?" he asked.

"I'm a student," I replied, glancing down at my feet, realizing he did not recognize me.

"Where do you go to school?"

"In Maryland," I replied.

"Oh, University of Maryland?"

"Ah, noooo … in Annapolis," I responded, drawing out my answer.

"St. John's?" he asked, hoping that I might be going to school down the street from him.

"No, I live down the hall from you," I said, forcing a smile across my face.

That was the moment our conversation ended, and he abruptly turned and walked away.

Male midshipmen brave enough to ask us out took the chance of being criticized by their classmates. "Can't find a real woman; got to date a mid?" To them, we were not considered "real women." Real women were the ones who did not attend the Academy and that men dated on the weekends. They wore makeup, fancy dresses, and sometimes elegant furs to football games in the hope of attracting the attention of a male midshipman. The men reciprocated by buying large yellow mum corsages to give to the women. A woman who wore her yellow mum on her lapel marked herself as "girlfriend of a mid." These were the "real women" I guess.

When another midshipman would ask us out, they would often say, "Just because I asked you out doesn't mean I believe women should be here." Imagine the contradiction in that message. While they did not appreciate or respect us as midshipmen, they did like that we were women.

Fortunately, not all men shied away from dating women midshipmen. I laud the ones who were able to see us as women as well as midshipmen. They were and are incredible men. Because dating a woman mid came with the certainty of being criticized by one's classmates, however, we sometimes dated in secret, knowing that if someone found out, it might mean the end of a relationship.

At the time, none of it made sense to me. I realize now that we were all young, and the times were confusing. In the late seventies and the early eighties, the Naval Academy was the bastion of naval tradition—a very male-centric tradition. Most of the men, being highly traditional themselves, were looking for women who were not challenging the status quo. They were looking for women who would follow them into their careers, not women who were intent on starting their own.

Eventually, we stopped telling people where we went to school. Like many of my female friends, for years I was reluctant to tell anyone where I had graduated from. Nearly a decade after graduation, I remember speaking with a friend from the Academy who shared that she still told people she went to a "small engineering college on the East Coast."

Crazy, isn't it? We went on to talk about how the negative messages we received at the Academy continued to affect us later in our lives. Then, we started laughing because deep down we knew that being a female Naval Academy graduate is really quite remarkable. As women, we need to claim who we are and where we come from if we want to continue growing throughout life. Be proud of who you are and what it took to get where you are today.

BE PROUD OF WHO YOU ARE AND WHAT IT TOOK TO GET WHERE YOU ARE TODAY.

In time, as we women midshipmen headed into the final stretch to graduate from the Academy, we came to a place of acceptance that we were both midshipmen and women. We would always be different than the men. Not only is that okay, but today, I find in my career and life that being a woman is actually quite exceptional.

The struggle to find one's identity is as old as time. Especially during our late teens and early twenties, we struggle to determine who we will be in the world. Following one's dream and finding one's identity are two intermingled challenges.

Many women in the workplace today still face the same challenge that we women midshipmen faced some forty years ago—the desire to be seen as women and as equals. Why can't you be a woman and still be seen as a man's equal? You can. But it can be a challenge. From how we dress to how we speak, criticism still abounds. But more and more women are finding their stride, showing the world that we can be both.

I recently asked Karen, my Academy roommate, what one piece of advice she would give women today. "Stay true to yourself and keep your standards high," she said. "Because in the end, you need to live with yourself."

Don't shy away from the struggle; it is important. Wrestling with ourselves is part of the process of growing into who we are becoming. We are always on that journey.

STAND UP AND SPEAK OUT

Four years at the Naval Academy is a grueling experience for anyone, from the academics and the military requirements to the physical, emotional, and mental challenges. We had it coming from all sides. And for the women, we had the added burden of, well, being women.

But there were men who were harassed as well. One situation that always stands out in my mind is when several upperclassmen in my company aimed their displeasure at one of my male classmates. We were second class (juniors), and the first class (seniors) picked on him for every slight infraction they could find, giving him more and more demerits. His room was not perfect, or his PE clothes were not removed from the hallway (that is where we put them to dry out in the sweltering Annapolis heat). I do not know why they singled him out. Perhaps it was because he was quite smart in unconventional ways. Or maybe it was because he was a little bit goofy and he was a friend of ours (me, Millie, and Karen). Over time, their nearly constant criticism of him began to affect not only him and his grades, but the overall morale within our company.

Our company commander called the second classmen together to inquire about why morale was suffering. "What's going on?" he asked.

The room fell silent.

This classmate was an engineering major like I was, and second-class year is the most academically challenging, especially for engineers, so I understood the pressure he was under. It is the "make or break" year with the most difficult courses, and success in these courses determines whether you will remain in your major. My classmate did not need or deserve the extra harassment he was receiving.

It seemed the elephant in the room was standing on my toes. It was time to speak up. "The first classmen are harassing our classmate," I said, my voice loud and clear. "It needs to stop. It is unfair and is affecting his performance."

The company commander looked shocked—I think not only because a woman had spoken up, but also because, as our leader, he did not know what was going on. I stood even taller as I went over the details of the situation, knowing that unit cohesion and morale had to be improved. My classmates smiled in approval.

The commander, a first classman himself, took action with his own classmates. He directed that all the harassment be stopped, and slowly morale improved. At our graduation a year and a half later, that same classmate's mother thanked me for standing up for her son. She said it made a big difference for him.

I KNOW THAT WHILE I CANNOT CHANGE THE WORLD, I CAN CHANGE MY PIECE OF IT.

Through my time at the Naval Academy, I learned that I cannot fight all the battles. But I can be selective in the ones I do fight, speak out and hold my ground. To this day, I know that while I cannot change the world, I can change my piece of it.

We need to remember to stand up for others as well as ourselves. Sometimes these issues fall under the radar, and the leaders don't know what is happening in their organizations. Inform them. Unfair treatment of others must always be stopped. It wears on everyone. Speak up and be the one who makes the difference.

EYE ON THE PRIZE

As we worked our way through the Academy, we eventually found ourselves as first-class midshipmen or seniors. Some of our struggles lifted, as if a cloud layer was clearing. Not that it was easy by any means, but we were starting to see ourselves graduating and becoming officers.

The women had not been completely accepted, but we had found our stride, and the finish line was coming into view. I recently asked my Academy roommate Karen what she remembers most about our latter years at the Academy. She said, "Our singular focus on graduation; that's what I remember."

The skies were not yet clear for me, though. I was a systems engineering major, and the additional credit hours required to get my engineering degree intensified my personal load. Many engineering programs at other universities extend beyond four years to accommodate the requirements for an engineering degree. But at the Naval

Academy, you have only four years to do the work. As a result, engineering majors carried between eighteen and twenty-two credit hours per semester, not including physical education.

Nonetheless, I wanted my engineering degree and was willing to put in the extra hours, which meant weekend studying, late nights at the library, and more time in the labs. I was building my grit and determination with each extra hour I studied. I knew my systems engineering degree would serve me well for the rest of my career, and that has certainly been my experience. Today, I tell my students that a STEM degree will be worth the personal investment and will ultimately take them places they never before imagined.

During that first-class year, I was invited to meet the first woman pilot to graduate from Navy Test Pilot School, Lt. Colleen Nevius. Not only was Colleen a test pilot; she was also one of the first women helicopter pilots in the Navy and one of the first women to complete a full deployment on a Navy ship. So when the invitation came, was I excited? You bet!

Lt. Carol Pottenger was one of only two women company officers at the Academy. When she invited the women who were interested in aviation to her home to meet Lt. Nevius, we were thrilled. Lt. Pottenger was one of the first women in the Navy to become qualified as a surface warfare officer (or ship driver as we say more informally), so she definitely caught our attention. Many women across the brigade looked up to her as a role model. We watched her every move. She was a lighthouse to us, flashing reminders of whom we might become in our futures.

Throughout my naval career, I paid attention and watched as Carol ultimately rose to the rank of vice admiral, commanding multiple ships and major military organizations never before commanded by a woman. As the commander of Amphibious Force, US 7th Fleet, she was the first woman to take charge of a Navy Expeditionary Strike Group, which is one of the most powerful collections of naval force in the world—three cruiser-destroyer ships, a submarine, and a Marine Expeditionary Unit. She was then, and remains today, remarkable to me.

To be invited to meet Colleen at Carol's home is a treasured memory I will never forget. Carol and Colleen were friends from Navy ROTC (Reserve Officers Training Corps) at Purdue University. You could feel the warmth and connection between them. Carol introduced Colleen with a knowing smile, as this woman definitely had something to say. I was immediately enamored by these two women several years senior to me, making their own marks in the Navy.

At the PAX River Naval Air Museum's "Women in Aviation" exhibit opening with Colleen and Carol

I leaned in as Colleen spoke about how to make yourself competitive for Test Pilot School (TPS), which is where the best of the best aviators go to become test pilots, test flight officers, and flight test engineers. TPS is a gateway to becoming an astronaut. In most cases, in order to become a pilot astronaut, you must graduate from either Navy Test Pilot School, Air Force Test Pilot School, or one of the two European test pilot schools. The Mercury Astronauts graduated from TPS, and still today many astronauts are graduates of Navy Test Pilot School.

I had never thought about TPS before that evening. Listening to Colleen, something grabbed me by surprise—I could combine my engineering degree with flying! In addition to possessing a solid engineering or technical background, we needed to follow Colleen's four key points if we wanted to make it into TPS.

"First, you will need to graduate at the top of your flight school class," Colleen shared, advising us that we needed to stand out among our peers from the beginning of our Navy careers and onward. "Then get one thousand hours of flight time and as many aircraft qualifications as you can as early as possible. Finally, tell every commanding officer you have that you want to go to TPS and that you will be asking them for letters of recommendation when you apply to the selection board."

Colleen's four points remain burned into my brain today. I used them throughout my Navy career, counseling others who wanted to go to TPS. I believe four equivalent points still exist for today's women who want to get to the top of their field:

1. Graduate at the top of your class.

2. Get as much experience under your belt as possible. At one hundred hours, we gain confidence in our abilities. At one thousand hours, we are proficient. At ten thousand hours, as bestselling author Malcom Gladwell says,[5] we achieve mastery.

---

5   Malcom Gladwell refers to the 10,000-hour rule as a way to achieve success multiple times in his book, *Outliers*.

3. Earn any available qualifications in your field.

4. Tell your teachers, bosses, and mentors what you want to do in your future (e.g., get your MBA or PhD, become a CEO, etc.) and ask them for help.

Learning to "fly" in any career or endeavor requires many hours of hard work and diligence. Follow these four points as you build your foundation, and it will serve you well.

That memorable night passed in a flash, and soon it was time to head back to the Academy. As we said our goodbyes, Colleen gave us parting words of advice. "I did it, and you can too!"

As I made the drive home, my mind was racing. I went back over everything Colleen had shared and began to think about the new possibilities. Pulling through the gates of the Academy, I looked at the Severn River in front of me, and in that moment, I knew what I wanted in my future beyond flight school: Navy Test Pilot School.

> **LEARNING TO "FLY" IN ANY CAREER OR ENDEAVOR REQUIRES MANY HOURS OF HARD WORK AND DILIGENCE.**

BRIDGE TO THE FUTURE

By late January of our first-class year, it was time for Service Selection Night. This was the evening when first-class midshipmen formally elected to become either naval officers or Marine Corps officers and selected the career path they would follow after graduation.

Midshipmen who were fully medically qualified and chose to become naval officers selected unrestricted line officer careers in aviation (pilot or naval flight officer), submarines, surface warfare, or special operations (Navy SEAL—these selections had extremely limited billets). Those not fully medically qualified selected jobs in the restricted line, with careers such as supply officer, engineer in the Civil Engineering Corps, or intelligence officer. Midshipmen who elected to become Marine Corps officers selected starting dates for The Basic School, where newly commissioned Marine Corps officers learned the fundamentals of being a Marine.

Service Selection Night was always charged with electricity as hopeful and anxious midshipmen selected their futures based entirely on class rank. The process is different now, but back then your future career path was determined on that one night, after four years spent at the Academy.

Of course, there was a bit of jostling that went on before Service Selection Night. During the upperclassman years, you learned where you fit in the pecking order and if your class rank would allow you the opportunity to follow the career path you wanted.

Generally, if you were in the top half of your class, you would get what you wanted. Aviation slots, however, were limited and coveted, so they went quickly. If you did not get an aviation career, you likely ended up in surface warfare as there were far more ships than planes available. If you wanted a submarine career, you had to be prescreened and interviewed ahead of time. Special ops slots were very few and always went early in the process.

Due to the combat exclusion laws, the opportunities for women were limited. Only a handful of unrestricted line officer slots (pilot, naval flight officer, and surface warfare) were available to women and were restricted to noncombatant ships and aircraft. Submarines and special ops were off the table, of course.

As women, we sought out information on each other's career goals so we knew the details surrounding everyone's ranking and which career they might select. For example, if a higher-ranked woman selected a coveted and limited intelligence officer slot, it meant another woman would not get that opportunity. If it seems that it was a bit competitive, it was.

The process that occurred on Service Selection Night was similar to the NFL draft, except the "draftees" selected where they would go. The top-ranked midshipman selected first, choosing a date for follow-on school for their desired career, a particular ship, or a specific location. The second-ranked midshipman selected second, and so on. Once all available slots were taken, for example in aviation, you had to choose another path. The "anchor man," the last-ranked midshipman, got the leftovers. No one wanted that position. This selection process was far different than anything in civilian life. If you chose a naval career path and did not like it, it was difficult, although not impossible, to change.

What shocked me the most that year was that several of the limited aviation slots for women would not be filled. Maybe it was the fact that aviation came with an additional commitment to the Navy—five years *after* getting your wings (which alone takes anywhere from one to two years) as opposed to just the standard five-year commitment. Or perhaps it was because many women had simply had enough, or they chose to veer away from a career that would guarantee they remained in a distinct minority.

I, on the other hand, was continuing on a grand adventure.

During my time at the Academy, I had developed my plan—my "flight plan." Initially, I went to the Naval Academy to get the education I desired. As a plebe, I had no idea what it meant to be a naval officer; however, as I became immersed in the culture of the military, I began to see myself as one. I engaged with men and women (but mostly men) who had chosen a military career, and I began to learn about the lives of service they had chosen to lead. The more I discovered, the more I knew that was what I wanted for my life as well.

When my number was called on Service Selection Night, it was an exhilarating feeling. I was starting my future as a commissioned officer. By then I knew with all my being that aviation was what I wanted. I had considered other opportunities before that night, but I always came back to flying. Perhaps it was the manifestation of the flying dreams I had so many years ago. It certainly felt that way.

Although I did not have the twenty-twenty eyesight required to become a pilot, my twenty-thirty vision was enough to become a naval flight officer.[6] Since I was in the top 15 percent of my class, I excitedly selected naval flight officer as my career choice and chose the flight school class date in Pensacola, Florida. I would still become an aviator!

Although I would have preferred to be a pilot, sometimes in life we have to change our flight plans. Some might consider a secondary plan as "less than" or as having to settle. Do not buy into that thinking. We are never "less than." It is the stories we tell ourselves that limit us. Had I gone through my career thinking that I was "less than" a pilot, I would have done tremendous damage to myself.

Sometimes the alternate path is the right one for us, even if we cannot see that at the time. Be willing to change your flight plan if necessary and embrace the change.

BE WILLING TO CHANGE YOUR FLIGHT PLAN IF NECESSARY AND EMBRACE THE CHANGE.

On Service Selection Night, Millie chose to become a Marine Corps officer, while Karen selected surface warfare officer and her future ship. We were giddy with excitement that we would be leaving the challenges of the Academy behind us and forging new futures for ourselves and for the women who would follow us. It was bittersweet that we would be going our separate ways, but we knew that we would always be part of one another's lives.

---

6   Naval flight officers work hand in hand with the pilot and handle the communications, navigation, radar, and weapons systems on board the aircraft. Flight officers initiate checklists and communications with air traffic control. Pilots and flight officers coordinate closely to get the aircraft into the air.

With our futures selected, we grabbed our dancing shoes and ran over to Dahlgren Hall to grab a few beers with our classmates, listen to some music and dance the night away. I'll never forget when the song "Celebration" by Kool and the Gang came on. "Celebrate good times, come on! Let's celebrate!" You bet we celebrated!

LAUNCH!

The Naval Service[7] thrives on tradition, acts of recognition, and ceremony. Beginnings and endings, from sailor enlistments and officer commissioning ceremonies to funerals and retirements, are all celebrated in the Naval Service. Also included are special holidays, promotions, and changes of command. For each occasion, we pull out our dress uniforms, attach our ribbons and medals, shine our shoes, and prepare to celebrate.

It takes a week to graduate from the Academy—a fitting entrée into the life of a naval officer. Known as Commissioning Week, this is a time that serves as a tribute to four years of grueling challenge, as we leave behind the title of midshipmen and become officers in the military service.[8] Every class participates in Commissioning Week. The first three years feel like a dress rehearsal, getting ready to launch

---

7   The Naval Service comprises both the Navy and the Marine Corps.

8   Upon graduation, midshipmen are commissioned as Navy ensigns or Marine Corps second lieutenants.

beyond the Academy and into the fleet. Then, in the fourth year, the final performance awaits.

Graduation at the Naval Academy is pomp and circumstance at its finest. Both exhilarating and exhausting, every graduate remembers it well. The week starts with the plebe recognition ceremony (the Herndon monument climb[9]), then shifts to parades with Navy bands, formal dances, special awards ceremonies, musical performances, the Blue Angels air show,[10] and the final Color Parade. As I write this, I can almost hear the timbre of the naval parade, the beating of the drums, the marching of footsteps, the low calling of cadences to keep everyone in step. I can feel the thunder of the Blue Angels overhead and the booming volleys of military gun salutes.

Finally, the culmination of the week and of four long years—graduation and commissioning as officers. The demanding pace, the music, the embrace of those loved ones who have come to celebrate, and the acrid smell of Annapolis humidity seem to stretch you one last time. Then suddenly, you are a graduate. You are never a midshipman again. Of course, we can always go back to our alma maters for a visit, but it is different. We are no longer part of the student body but part of a larger community.

When I observe alumnae come back to where I work today, I see myself in their eyes. It is that look of knowing, of recognition of how the school helped launch them into their adult lives. I call it an inflection point of knowing that where we come from—including the trials, the challenges, the good, the bad, the ugly—stays with us for the rest of our lives.

Throughout graduation week of 1983, Millie, Karen, and I raced

---

9   A historic part of Academy tradition, as a class, plebes are tasked with climbing a greased Herndon monument and replacing a plebe's Dixie cap with a white officer's cover, signaling that the fourth classmen are no longer plebes.

10   The Blue Angels are the Navy's premier flight demonstration team.

from event to event, passing our classmates in the hallways and on the parade field, knowing but barely allowing ourselves to acknowledge the twist of emotions arising in us. Exhausted, enthralled, ecstatic, amazed, bewildered—it was an incredible mix.

Graduation morning, it was our last uniform race into our best dress white uniforms. We grabbed our midshipmen covers and the prized boxes that held our new officer covers. Before leaving the room, we stopped for a moment of reverence. This was our final day—as midshipmen and as roommates.

The football stadium, filled with a sea of white uniforms, was the site for graduation. No sunglasses were allowed, so the sun reflecting off our uniforms was absolutely blinding. One by one, we buoyantly marched across the stage as the vice president of the United States of America awarded our diplomas. There were fifty-three women and over one thousand men. We had all succeeded, but it was extra sweet to be one of the fifty-three! We had overcome infinitely more obstacles than the others, and we knew it.

AS I RECEIVED MY DIPLOMA, I THREW MY HANDS IN THE AIR AND SHOUTED ... I FELT TRIUMPHANT!

As I received my diploma, I threw my hands in the air and shouted. I do not remember exactly what I said, but I felt triumphant!

My dream had been to fly. My vision had been to pursue something bigger than myself, and that vision led me to the Naval Academy. Soon I would discover just how far that dream and vision would take me.

A mile of highway will take you a mile.
A mile of runway will take you anywhere!
—AUTHOR UNKNOWN

FIND YOUR WINGS

Below are some questions to get you thinking about where you are now and where you want to be in the future. My hope is that these thought starters will help you identify your goals and dreams and chart a course to achieve them. Visit www.captainbarbarabell.com to download a free tool to help you create your own "flight plan."

WHAT IS THE VISION YOU HAVE FOR YOURSELF? WHAT IS YOUR RUNWAY?

WHAT ARE YOUR DREAMS?

Are they front and center, or have you forgotten them? Take some time to really think about your dreams. What did you dream of early in your life? What is your current dream? What is the vision you have for yourself? What is your runway?

WHAT ARE YOUR POSSIBILITIES?

Don't limit yourself, especially when you are young. Explore the world. Collect your own "brown bags" of opportunity. There are hundreds of options out there. Consider all the possibilities—you may be amazed by what you find.

HOW ARE YOU DEVELOPING GRIT?

Grit is built through struggle; there is no way around it. What situations have you faced in the past that have already helped you develop tenacity? Can you seek out new challenges to help you further grow your fortitude and determination?

WHO IS YOUR SUPPORT SYSTEM?

None of us do this thing called life alone. Who is on your team that will support you and help you through challenging times? Who are your sisters (or your brothers)? Find other women (or men) you can connect with and provide support to, and who can provide support to you.

DO YOU HAVE YOUR EYE ON THE PRIZE?

At one thousand hours, we are experienced and proficient. What does "getting your hours" mean in the context of your career? How many hours have you already logged?

PART TWO:
NAVIGATING
TURBULENCE

I refused to take no for an answer.
—BESSIE COLEMAN,
First Black woman and first American Indian to
earn a pilot license, June 15, 1921

STRAP IN

How many times have you flown on a commercial aircraft, and midflight the captain announces there is turbulence ahead and asks you to return to your seat and put on your seat belt? You hear the familiar chime as the seat belt sign illuminates above your head. You strap in and pull that seat belt just a bit tighter. And then you wait.

Soon the turbulence begins. The plane begins to shake (and maybe you do too). The flight attendants lurch in the aisle. Your drink sloshes on the tray table. You might even get a bit of a queasy feeling in your stomach. As the turbulence grows stronger and your grip tightens on the armrests you think, "When will we get through this?"

For a passenger or even a pilot in training, turbulence can be unnerving. But have you noticed that when you are expecting it, it does not seem as unsettling? That is why the captain announces it—so that you will be prepared.

Aviators know that turbulence is nothing more than rough air. We understand why it happens and where it is coming from. We know we can simply climb or descend or fly around it until we find smooth air.

We don't have to stay in the turbulence. This is a great life lesson.

Turbulence happens in life as well. We all experience it—perhaps not in the same form, but we all hit rough patches. Whenever we leave the ground and "take it into the air," we are going to experience challenges, obstacles, and difficulties. If you want to soar, you are going to go through some "turbulence." It might come in the form of criticism of you or your dreams, harassment, microaggressions, resistance, etc. It is not a question of *if* it will happen; it is merely a question of *when.*

WE DON'T HAVE TO STAY IN THE TURBULENCE.

So what do you do when you find yourself in a bit of turbulence?

Buckle up. Strap in. Prepare yourself. Know that you can work your way around or through any obstacle that arises. The more experience you get, the more comfortable you will become with the turbulence of life. You will learn to relax and move forward with confidence, knowing you are just going through a rough patch and that smooth air awaits you on the other side.

As difficult as the Naval Academy had been for me, I was prepared for more challenges ahead. But as I graduated and headed to flight school, I knew I was taking a multitude of hard-earned skills with me, and I was ready to navigate the coming turbulence.

DON'T SKIP FLIGHT SCHOOL

Known as the "cradle of naval aviation," Pensacola, Florida, is where all future Navy and Marine Corps aviators begin their careers. I made the trip from Annapolis to Pensacola with my classmate, Lisa, who was also going to flight school and would be my roommate. After the one-thousand-mile drive, we arrived at Pensacola pier, taking in the sights of Pensacola Bay and the Navy base beyond.

As we stepped out of our cars, we heard the looming sound of jet engines. Looking up, hearts beating and half expecting what we might see, the Blue Angels zoomed by in formation! The sound was deafening. Thrilled, we threw our hands up in the air and yelled. We knew it was a sign: we were going to be Naval aviators!

I was ready for Navy Flight School before it even started. I had begun working on my private pilot's license during my last semester at the Naval Academy and had flown small Cessna 150s and 152s in the skies surrounding the Naval Academy and along the Eastern Shore of Maryland. Cessnas were my first real taste of flight. They were like Matchbox cars in comparison to the "Ferrari" Navy aircraft, but they were a start. I finished my private pilot's license in Pensacola the day before flight school started, but I was already thinking about flying jets.

Becoming an aviator (whether Navy, Air Force, commercial, or recreational) requires a great deal of knowledge and skill. In the Navy, prospective aviators attend Navy Flight School, which includes three components:

1. Aviation Preflight Indoctrination ("API")—the initial "preflight" training, which covers the basics of flight mechanics, propulsion, and land and water survival.

2. Ground School—the knowledge portion of training, when prospective aviators learn aeronautics (the physics of how airplanes fly), navigation, communications, and weather. Aviators spend a lot of time in ground school. Yes, learning to fly the aircraft is the ultimate goal, but there is a lot of work that must go into training on the ground first.

3. Flight Training—the actual skills of flying an airplane, including taking off and landing, flight planning, various maneuvers, and how to handle emergencies.

Aviators go through several iterations of ground school and flight training in three phases: basic, intermediate, and advanced, learning more complex topics and skills each time. I attended flight school multiple times throughout my career because certification in each new aircraft typically requires another round of ground school and flight training.

In life as in aviation, we need knowledge and training before we take flight.

I think of learning as the ground school of life. We grow our knowledge through school, reading, life experiences, and personal and professional development. The Naval Academy was the ground school of my life. It is where I began to develop the foundation that would support the rest of my life and career.

Skills training and practice are equally as important as expanding our knowledge. Job experiences, working with a mentor, developing a support system—all of these will help you learn to maneuver through your career and handle whatever challenges might come your way.

During ground school in Pensacola, we learned about the environmental factors

IN LIFE AS IN AVIATION, WE NEED KNOWLEDGE AND TRAINING BEFORE WE TAKE FLIGHT.

that affect weather and how to read the clouds. "Are those cumulus, cirrus, stratus, nimbus or cumulonimbus clouds out there?" our instructors would ask. We learned what produces a thunderstorm and how to avoid one. We learned never to fly into or under a thunderstorm, always around or on top. Our instructors frequently reminded us that flying can be unpredictable, and it is always best to be prepared.

Life too can be unpredictable. Some days the clouds roll in, the weather gets bumpy, and your sightlines become obscured. You may lose track of the horizon and your vision in the midst of challenge. Those are the times to reconnect with your knowledge, training, and support system. If you have built a strong foundation, you will be able to weather life's storms.

The flight school of life is not a "one and done." Career changes, life changes, unexpected obstacles—these are the situations when you might need to go back to the basics for a while, do another round of learning and training. Revisit your dream and continue to build your foundation. Before you know it, you'll be flying high in a new direction.

"NO" IS A COMPLETE SENTENCE

After checking into Naval Air Station Pensacola, I reported to flight school, only to discover that my class start date was delayed by three weeks. (Lisa's start date ended up being delayed for several months, so she was in another group.) It is not unusual for flight school start dates to be delayed as the training command attempts to sequence students through the multiple phases of flight training. Weather and aircraft maintenance can also play havoc with the schedule.

For short delays such as mine, students had to show up every two days, stand in formation to be counted as present, and then be dismissed. Most headed to the beach. Longer delays might mean a temporary assignment somewhere else on base. Disappointed that I could not start right away, I thought some beach time with my friends might not be too bad. To my surprise, I was assigned a job nearly immediately.

Unbeknownst to me at the time but revealed to me later, a single Marine captain flight instructor had noticed me as the only woman in ranks and thought it would be a great idea if I worked for him for a few weeks. Perhaps he thought it might lead to something more. Who knows? Unhappy that my male classmates were headed to the beach, I reported to his office.

After introducing myself as Ensign Bell, he asked me two questions that I will remember for the rest of my life. First, he asked me if I could *type*. (Remember, it was the early eighties.) Really? I had just graduated from the United States Naval Academy, and this guy wanted to know if I could type?

Crazy responses flew through my head. "What planet are you on? Obviously not the same one as me!" "Are you serious?" With my fury building, I thought, "Who the @#$! do you think you are?" Then I remembered he was senior to me.

Luckily, my time at the Academy taught me how to control my emotions, so the words in my head did not immediately come out of my mouth. Perhaps it was the conditioning from my plebe year and the five basic responses we were allowed to give when questioned.

I collected my thoughts, then responded, "Sir, the reason I joined the Navy is to fly. If I had to type for a living, I would starve to death. I don't type, sir."

I had learned at the Academy that you can say nearly anything as long as you say it in a respectful manner and finish your sentences with either "sir" or "ma'am." Thinking that might be enough to satisfy him, I was flabbergasted by his next question.

"Well, can you make coffee?" He added, "You will be responsible for making coffee each day."

As a graduate of the United States Naval Academy, I was not going to make anyone's coffee. Again, my Naval Academy training took over, and I responded appropriately.

"I do not drink coffee, and I do not make coffee, sir," I said emphatically.

He had no idea what to do with me at that point. Was this sexual harassment? Maybe. Was he challenging boundaries? Most definitely. However, I was clear: I was in Pensacola to go to flight school; not to type, not to make coffee, and certainly not to go out on a date with a single Marine captain.

I worked for him for three short weeks. Our work relationship, though professional, remained a bit awkward. My hope is that he learned something from me just as I did from him. I hope he learned from me to respect women as professionals, not denigrate them as personal assistants. For me, it was another lesson in knowing and holding my boundaries.

Today, you may not be asked if you can type or make coffee, but you may be asked to do something beneath your skill set. You may be asked to order lunch, plan the next office party, or take notes at the next meeting, when no man or colleague is asked to do the same.

At some point in your career, your boundaries will be challenged. Be ready. Know and keep your boundaries, both professional and personal. Be clear about why you are doing what you have chosen to do and hold fast. As my friend Kim teaches, "Your boundaries are yours and no one else's—just as clear as the nose on your face."

KNOW AND KEEP YOUR BOUNDARIES, BOTH PROFESSIONAL AND PERSONAL.

Although we may be angry (or even afraid) when our boundaries are challenged, it is important we take a moment to collect ourselves in order to respond appropriately rather than react emotionally. Use humor or just give a direct no. I tell women whom I mentor, "'No' is a complete sentence."

For all you grammarians out there, I do not want to debate whether "No" is a complete sentence. The point is that when we say no, we often feel we must explain ourselves or justify our response. I think this is especially true for women. Sometimes we get wrapped up in long-winded rationalizations because inwardly we feel we need to say yes even when we want to say no. But no explanation or justification is necessary.

I laughed out loud when I read that author and former executive Shelly Tygielski says, "Learning to say 'no' and letting it hang out there all alone in its glory is a small kind of superpower."[11] Indeed it is a superpower! When we set and protect our boundaries, we usually find they are respected.

Recognize too that sometimes protecting your boundaries means walking away. I mentioned earlier that my time at the Naval Academy taught me that I had to be selective in the battles I chose to fight. Not all battles can be won. Just because you *can* engage does not necessarily mean you should. Had I fought all the battles that came my way, I would have only become hardened, angry, and exhausted. Always stand up for yourself, but don't become hardened in the process.

---

11   Shelly Tygielski, "'No' Is a Complete Sentence," mindful.org, January 16, 2019, https://www.mindful.org/no-is-a-complete-sentence/.

GO DEEPER ... THEN SURFACE

Finally, it was time to start flight school!

Aviation Preflight Indoctrination was the first step to becoming naval aviators. API taught us the fundamentals of flight—lift, weight, thrust, and drag. In our propulsion class, we studied the engines that would provide the thrust for our aircraft and learned the differences between propeller engines, turbo-prop engines, and jet engines. As an engineering graduate, I found these classes were not too difficult.

The navigation classes were similar to the navigation classes I took at the Academy, except that an aircraft, of course, goes much faster than a ship. In the air, you must know not only where you are at all times but also where you are going and how much fuel is required to get there. As aviation students, we were pushed to think faster, to look farther ahead, and to maintain our situational awareness ("SA") at all times.

The real fun began with water survival training. In the Navy, we mostly fly over water—over the bay, over the ocean near the coast, or over the open ocean (called "blue water ops") where there is no alternate landing field other than the aircraft carrier. Water survival training is crucial.

First, we learned to escape from a simulated underwater crash situation by training in an underwater cockpit escape device, nicknamed the "Dilbert Dunker."[12] If you have seen the classic movie *An Officer and a Gentleman,* you may remember the famous Dilbert Dunker scene. Students are strapped into an aircraft seat in an engineering contraption somewhat resembling an aircraft cockpit. The "cockpit" is then rolled down a track at a forty-five-degree angle at speeds up to twenty-five miles per hour until it plummets into a swimming pool. Once it hits the water, it tumbles over once, and it comes to rest inverted near the bottom of the pool.

Crazy? Yes. However, it is critical survival training, and it is a rite of passage for all aviators.

The adventure is a great lesson in anxiety control. Once "all motion stops" (as I clearly remember our instructor saying), we were instructed to release ourselves from the seat, swim toward the *bottom* of the pool to move away from the simulated "burning aircraft," and then and only then, turn and follow our air bubbles to the surface of the pool.

As we lined up for our turn in the dunker with hearts racing, we tried not to show our fear. The class got quiet ... very quiet. The tension was palpable.

My class of twenty included only two women. The other woman, an All-American swimmer, asked to go first. "I'll lose my nerve if I don't go right away," she uttered, nervously tapping a thigh.

"An All-American swimmer nervous?" I gulped to myself.

---

12   "The Birth of the Dilbert Dunker," navalaviationmuseum.org, accessed November 18, 2021, https://www.navalaviationmuseum.org/history-up-close/objects-of-history/birth-dilbert-dunker/.

She easily succeeded, and soon all eyes were on me.

I tried to remain cool on the outside as my anxiety was building inside. Taking several deep breaths in anticipation of going underwater, I was grateful for my experience as a swimmer and the years I spent as a child swimming in the summer. The simulated cockpit released with a loud "clunk," and seconds later, holding a big gulp of air, I crashed into the pool. Heart racing, flipping head over heels, I reminded myself that I was experiencing what hundreds of aviators had done before me.

With my sinuses filling with water, I knew what to do as both a swimmer and runner—regulate my breath. I held my breath to calm myself, then released it slowly. I had a sense of seeing clearly. I had been in cold water before, lots of it in fact, in northern Michigan.

Time expanded as I waited for "all motion to stop." Now I could see the wisdom in our instructor's advice. By waiting for all motion to stop, I was able to stay connected to the situation, rather than panicking and adding to the chaos. Moving my hand down the webbing of the harness, I located and pulled the quick release. Defying instinct to immediately head to the surface, I swam just a bit deeper into the pool, then turned toward the light and swam to the surface. As I popped up, a smile spread across my face. My rite of passage was complete.

My triumph was short lived. Yet another water survival adventure awaited us—one that made our ride in the Dilbert Dunker seem like a splash in an infant pool.

The "Helo Dunker," more affectionately known as "Panic in a Drum," simulates a helicopter crash landing into water. The simulator looks like a gigantic tin can that holds six aircrew—two in the cockpit and four in the cargo space. There are cutouts on the "can" to simulate blown-out windscreens and an open cargo door. The "can" is held above the pool by pivot attachments at each end.

Once everyone is onboard and strapped in, the "can" is dropped into the pool, then rotated to simulate a helicopter flipping upside down when it hits the water. The exercise requires students to get out of the "helicopter" and find their way to the surface. The technique used to escape is essentially the same as the Dilbert Dunker: wait until all motion stops, first go deeper, and then swim to the surface.

The really fun part is that students get to ride the Helo Dunker four times. Yes, count them—*one, two, three, four* times. The first two rides simulate day operations; the second two, night conditions where you have to escape blindfolded. As if four times isn't enough, this training is required again in subsequent years to recertify as an aviator.

Recently, my Academy roommate Millie remarked that I approached work and life in quite a calm manner. Maybe some of my calmness stems from the training I've had, especially water survival training. Since my flight training in Pensacola, I've been dunked quite a few times by life—the loss of a relationship, a job that did not work out, the graduate school acceptance I was certain I would receive but didn't.

WHEN LIFE GETS CRAZY ... WE NEED TO "WAIT UNTIL ALL MOTION STOPS" AND THEN "GO DEEPER."

What I have come to realize is that losses usually turn into new opportunities that lead us in a direction never before imagined. But the anxiety or sadness in those moments has the potential to stop our forward progress. Over time, I've learned that when life gets crazy and our anxiety starts to get the best of us, we need to "wait until all motion stops" and then "go deeper." Pause and take some time away from the situation. Maybe it is a few minutes, maybe a day or even a few weeks. Let the chaos subside so you can examine the situation and think clearly.

Perhaps you have a major life decision to make, as I did several years ago. I went away by myself, allowing the chaos in my head to clear. With time to go more deeply within myself, I was able to calmly examine my situation and my emotions and determine where I wanted to go in my life. I found the decision I needed to make.

Anxiety can also come from the smaller daily issues of life. "Wait and go deeper" works here as well. Perhaps as a parent it means giving yourself a "time out" before engaging again with your children after a frustrating conversation. I know that stepping away and catching my breath allows me to examine my emotions and then to respond to the situation instead of reacting to it.

The more practiced we become with facing our anxiety, the less it has a hold on us. Remember, wait until all motions stops, go deeper by going further into the experience, and then push through the anxiety and rise to the surface.

GEAR UP

By the time water survival training transitioned to para-sailing and swimming a mile in our flight suits, we began to think we were actually having fun. Our intense preflight training introduced us to a whole new world, that of military aviation. We had crossed a threshold, progressing to the next phase of training.

An essential element of learning to fly is acquiring the equipment and tools that enable pilots to perform at their peak. In flight training, before we even climbed into our aircraft, we put on our flight gear.

Navy jet flight gear includes a flight suit, steel-toed flight boots, a "G suit,"[13] helmet, oxygen mask, and integrated torso harness that straps us into our aircraft, into our ejection seat, and into our

---

13   A "G suit" or more specifically, an antigravity suit, is worn by aviators to counteract the pooling of blood that occurs in the lower extremities when under significant "g-forces" and to keep blood flowing to the brain, preventing loss of consciousness.

parachute. This specialized seat belt also includes carefully selected survival gear, such as a life jacket, flashlight, radio, shroud cutter, mirror, whistle, water, day/night flares, and during combat missions, a pistol.

Putting on all my flight gear was a bit overwhelming at first—a bit claustrophobic in fact—but eventually it became like a second skin. Not only did my gear feel a part of me, but its use became second nature as well, which is extremely important.

Every pilot is keenly aware of the value of their flight gear. Flight gear supports us during the flight, and in the extreme case of having to eject from the aircraft, supports us for twenty-four hours of survival either on the ground or in the water. Linda, a naval aviator colleague, once had to eject from an EA-6A aircraft. She was flying over the Atlantic when her aircraft experienced a total hydraulic failure. Controllability of the aircraft was lost, so she and the pilot had to eject.

THERE IS "GEAR" FOR OUR PROFESSIONAL LIVES— EQUIPMENT AND TOOLS ... THAT SUPPORT US AND HELP US TO PERFORM AT OUR BEST.

Linda said she remembers pulling the ejection handle, seeing a flash of light (a rocket ignites within the ejection seat, sending the crewmember into the sky and clear of the aircraft) and the yellow note paper from her kneeboard flying around like confetti. She passed out momentarily, then came to with the tug of the opening parachute. Relying on her flight gear and following all her emergency procedures, which had become instinct by this time, she released the parachute as she entered the water, swam to her life raft, and fortunately was picked up by search and rescue about an hour later. Her flight gear saved her life. She had all the equipment she needed and knew how to use it when the time came.

Although we may not always be aware of it, there is "gear" for our professional lives—equipment and tools (both tangible and intangible) that support us and help us to perform at our best.

My friend Anna is an architect on large-scale construction projects. Recently we were speaking about "gearing up" for meetings and presentations, and I asked her how she prepares. "When I give a key presentation, I wear four-inch heels," she said. "I work in a predominantly male environment. When I wear heels, I can look most men in the eye." She went on to say, "I also create a larger presence by taking up a lot of physical space at a table." Well-known business executive and chief operating officer of Facebook Sheryl Sandburg talks about taking your seat at the table. Anna takes two!

What equipment and tools might you carry with you in your career?

- Flight suit—Do you wear clothes that are appropriate for the job and make you feel confident? Do you stand out for the right reasons? When I completed Naval Postgraduate School, the wife of one of my colleagues commented on seeing me at graduation. "As you walked across the stage, you looked different than the others. Your dress uniform fit perfectly; you walked with confidence; I knew it was you."

- Steel-toed boots—What protects you from "getting your toes stepped on"? Perhaps a healthy sense of humor or solid dose of self-assurance?

- Oxygen mask—Who or what sustains you and keeps you going when times get tough?

- Ejection seat—Do you have an "escape plan?" Have you identified your next goal for when it's time to move on to the next phase of your career?

- Radio—Do you have exceptional communication and interpersonal skills?

- Life jacket—Do you have a mentor or support system?

One of my favorite tools is humor. I use it often. Humor helps me defuse tense or uncomfortable situations, giving me time to figure out the exact tool that is needed next. Millie has said that she also uses humor to disarm opposition and to gain respect:

"When I was a captain in the Marine Corps, the colonel I reported to introduced me to another visiting colonel.

"He said, 'This is Captain G; she's a real asshole.'

"I said, 'Excuse me, sir?'

"Then he said, 'She doesn't take shit from anyone.'

"And I responded, 'If that's what an asshole is, then I'm a big one!'

"It was a pretty good reputation to have as a woman Marine. And it worked well for me as I navigated the corporate world."

Whether you refer to your "gear" as a toolbox, a backpack, or something else, the important thing is to have the tools you need to be successful. They must be readily accessible at a moment's notice to handle situations as they arise. This is how we develop ourselves as humans and, most certainly, as leaders.

OTHERS ARE WATCHING

Last year I visited Naval Air Station Pensacola with my daughter and friends, staying in a cottage on the beach. I had not been back to Pensacola in decades. As I awoke in the mornings to the sounds of aircraft engines humming in the distance, memories flooded my mind. One in particular kept coming back to me.

Early in flight school, I was pulled over one day by the base police for driving too fast on base. I was given a speeding ticket that came with an invitation to see the commanding officer of the base. "Crap! Why did I do that?" I wondered. This was not how Ensign Bell wanted to meet the commanding officer.

Pulling myself together in my polished shoes and crisp khakis and with not a hair out of place, I reported to his office a few days later. "You have to remember everyone is watching you," the captain exhorted. "You are one of the only women on base. You must be a role model." He said it with kindness and awareness that I was one of the few women in the Navy that chose to go into naval aviation, but the message was clear.

His point washed over me again and again. Everyone was watching me—from the most senior officer to the most junior enlisted sailor. Would I succeed? Would I fail? I wondered about how I conducted myself—in class, on the flight line, at the gym. Was I respectful to all with whom I came into contact?

I breathed in, then out, taking in the significance of his words. It became crystallized in my mind that I was in flight school not only for myself, but also to open the doors a bit further for all the women who would follow me.

The captain and I talked a bit more. Then he let me out of my ticket. Feeling relieved and grateful, I departed his office recognizing that he had helped me to see the importance of what I was doing. I was a role model for women in naval aviation whether I liked it or not. Good or bad, my actions and behavior would speak volumes to both the women and men around me.

I WAS A ROLE MODEL FOR WOMEN IN NAVAL AVIATION WHETHER I LIKED IT OR NOT.

I took the captain's advice to heart, and it has been a guiding principle in my life ever since. I decided that day that on the outside, I would always be polished. I tailored my uniforms, kept my shoes shined and my hair pulled back, and always stayed in good physical shape. On the inside, I would continue to develop my drive to become the kind of aviator with whom others wanted to fly. This didn't mean that I had to be perfect. I would make mistakes, as we all do. How I handled mistakes was where I would be watched even more closely, another way for me to shine.

Karen, my roommate from the Academy, understands the importance of being a role model. "I definitely strive to do my best and be the best in everything I do. I treat others the way that I want others to treat me, and I put the mission or job over self," she explained recently. "I believe that when you do these things, coworkers at all levels will respect you, and you can make a positive difference. I've had people who weren't direct reports come to me because they knew that I would help them or give them advice. When they would approach me, they would say that from observing me, they felt that I knew what I was doing, and it helped that I was also approachable. That made me feel that I was the example that I hoped to be."

Halfway through flight school, I was reminded again that I was a role model. A Black male lieutenant instructor took me aside to chat. He approached me with kindness and respect and passed on some hard-won wisdom from his own experiences. He explained that I would always stand out and that I would constantly be watched. He encouraged me to work hard, always be professional, and not to date any instructors, as that would signal to my male peers that I was trying to gain an advantage over them.

Throughout flight school, I did not date instructors, and in my early career when I was single, I did not date anyone in my squadron or in my chain of command. Regardless of the industry we work in, I believe as women we should never date someone who has power over us or that we have power over. *Never.* There are too many stories of downfall for those who have engaged in unequal power relationships. Men lose, and women often lose even more.

I appreciated that this lieutenant thought enough of who I was to mentor me. His words of encouragement reminded me that we women were not the first to break new ground in aviation. Black men had been aviation pioneers decades prior. The 99th Pursuit Squadron, which became known as the Tuskegee Airmen, was established in 1941 and was comprised of America's first Black military pilots. These amazing aviators faced racism both within and outside the armed forces. They had tremendous success during World War II and laid the groundwork for desegregation of the military.

It can be either a burden or a privilege to be a role model—it all depends on how you embrace it. The good news is that you get to choose. I chose to see it as a privilege. I hope that you will, too.

AVERAGE WON'T CUT IT

fter API, our larger flight school group split up into smaller groups for ground school. Those who would become pilots headed off to Whiting Field just north of Pensacola, while student naval flight officers stayed in Pensacola. For me it was Pensacola, where I reported to aviation squadron VT-10.

Ground school continued much like my previous classes, where they drilled into our heads the priorities of the air—aviate, navigate, and communicate. I've found these priorities are also fitting for our lives:

- Aviate—focus on what is right in front of you.

- Navigate—know where you are going.

- Communicate—let others know about your life and where you are going with it.

Before we were allowed in an actual aircraft, we spent hours in trainers and simulators to develop our flying skills. We employed flight checklists, from preflight checks to engine start to post-takeoff. We memorized emergency procedures—what to do when an engine shuts down, a hydraulic system stops working, or smoke enters the cockpit. We were learning how to become true flight crew members. Days were filled with instruction, tests, simulators, and more instruction. Nights at home were spent studying and practicing our skills.

Finally, we entered into the flight portion of our training. Up on deck was the T-34 trainer. Nothing like the Cessnas I had trained in for my private pilot license, the T-34 is a turboprop tandem-seat trainer. The instructor sits in front, while the student sits in the seat behind the instructor. Also unlike the Cessna, students wear full flight gear, including an oxygen mask, and are strapped into the aircraft. My first flight in the T-34 proved uneventful, and I discovered a knack for flying in a different way, as part of a crew rather than as an individual. Working together, the pilot and the naval flight officer maximize the potential of the aircraft and the systems onboard.

After our initial familiarization (or "fam") flights, it was on to primary, then intermediate and advanced phases of flight training. Flight school is a highly competitive environment. Each flight is graded, and your grade point average is continually compared against your classmates' average. Your grade point average determines whether you are selected to fly jets or propeller aircraft, with jets requiring higher grades than "props."

I knew I wanted to fly jets. Nothing else would do. I wanted to soar around in the sky—for short missions at rapid speed. I was not interested in the longer missions of propeller aircraft. "Drilling holes in the sky," as we used to say, for hours on end in reconnaissance flights, didn't appeal to me.

Partway through flight training, I surprisingly found myself in the middle of the pack—decent grades, but nothing spectacular. I had failed a flight like most students had, but I had picked myself up and gotten back on track. My performance was *average*. I had never in my life been average at something I set my mind to.

What had gone wrong?

I had gotten too comfortable, working hard enough to get by but not enough to distinguish myself. Perhaps after four years at the Naval Academy, I was "taking a break" from all-out intensity. I had also lost sight of my dream of going to Navy Test Pilot School.

It didn't feel good. Something needed to change. "Average" was not going to get me where I wanted to go. I needed to graduate at the top of my class. I decided to take action—to light a fire under my own butt and change my situation.

The more I thought about the issue, the more I thought about those priorities of the air that we learned in ground school. While I could aviate, navigate, and communicate in the aircraft, I was not doing so "at altitude" in my professional life.

Aviate was my first priority—refocusing on the task in front of me. The challenge was graduating at the top of my flight school class, not just my next flight. I determined that I needed a different approach to the remaining flights in my program. I began to see each flight not as a box to be checked on the syllabus, but as a stepping-stone toward my goal of finishing at the top.

Next I needed to *navigate* the challenge ahead, but this time with help.

Shortly thereafter, and quite serendipitously, I was assigned a mentor. He was an older, somewhat crusty lieutenant who was prior enlisted (meaning he started his career as a sailor before becoming an officer). Taking what I felt was a risk, as I had not even finished flight school yet, I *communicated* to my mentor that, ultimately, I wanted to go to Test Pilot School.

"I need to be a top performer!" I said.

He looked me directly in the eyes and told me in no uncertain terms that I was capable of graduating at the top of my flight school class. And he would help me.

My mentor challenged me to study extra hours each night. He urged me to go back to base after hours and do extra trainers and simulators the night before each flight. He tasked me with knowing my navigation charts so well that I could fly my flights with my eyes closed. He checked my knowledge and pushed me ever further. I ate it up. My grades improved dramatically, and I graduated at the top of my flight school class with the honors of "Commodore's List with Distinction."

If you find yourself in a place where you are not happy with your performance, do what it takes to change it.

IF YOU FIND ... YOU ARE NOT HAPPY WITH YOUR PERFORMANCE, DO WHAT IT TAKES TO CHANGE IT.

In the midst of the day-to-day work it takes to achieve our goals, sometimes we forget about our dreams. When your dream begins to wane, remember these three words: aviate, navigate, and communicate. Step into the challenge right in front of you, go find a mentor or a coach to help you problem solve, and continue to communicate your dreams to everyone who will listen. The right mentor at the right time can help you produce remarkable results. Follow their guidance and commit to the extra work. It will pay off.

GIFTS OFTEN COME IN
UNEXPECTED PACKAGES

As was Navy tradition at the time, the top graduate in each flight school class was given their choice of aircraft to fly, which dictated where you would be stationed and where your future career path might lead. Well, that was, unless you were a woman. That's what I call the "fine print." The "tradition" applied only to men.

Although women could go to fight school, they could not be assigned to operational squadrons (e.g., squadrons that might go into combat). The "fine print" was the combat exclusion laws that prevented women from flying combat aircraft in operational squadrons and from serving on combatant ships. Women could only be assigned to support squadrons that trained or supported operational squadrons and aircraft carriers. (Years later, I would work with other women on Capitol Hill to repeal these laws. More on that later.)

Bottom line, although I graduated at the top of my class, I was not given my first choice of aircraft. Navy tradition did not apply to me. Instead, I was assigned the A-3 Skywarrior, an antiquated Vietnam War–era aircraft. It was the same aircraft that the two men at the bottom of my flight school class were assigned.

Career limiting? Yes. Disappointed? Yes. Defeated? No.

As a consolation prize, I was given the choice of which squadron I wanted, either on the East Coast or the West Coast. Considering my two options, the notes to the song "California Dreamin'" filtered through my brain. "I'll take California," I said with a wink, choosing squadron VAQ-34, in Pt. Mugu, just north of Los Angeles.

With no idea of what an A-3 looked like, I sheepishly asked for some guidance. "What is an A-3 by the way?"

I don't remember which instructor responded, but I do remember what he said. "If you go to the Naval Aviation Museum, out back where they don't mow the grass around the aircraft anymore, you will find one."

I headed over to the museum, swallowing my pride as I went. Dragging my feet as I slowly walked out the back of the museum, I peered over the high, unkempt grass. Just as the instructor indicated, there it stood—the mighty A-3. She was big, old, and a bit unloved, but she was my future. "Well, here we go." I sighed.

But something unexpected happened.

As it turned out, flying the A-3 offered everything I needed in pursuit of Test Pilot School. Although I would fly the A-3 in a support squadron, the A-3 was also an operational aircraft in the US fleet. Nicknamed "the whale," the A-3 was big and ugly for sure, but it was respected on aircraft carriers. I would go on to fly with combat-trained aviators, some of them Vietnam War veterans, and learn much from them.

Sometimes gifts come in unusual and unexpected packages.

If you are assigned to a project or offered an opportunity that on the surface seems less than desirable, don't despair. Jump in, do your best, and be wholeheartedly committed. Unwrap the gift that has been given to you. You might be amazed with what is inside.

SOMETIMES GIFTS COME IN UNUSUAL AND UNEXPECTED PACKAGES.

After leaving the Marine Corps, Millie went on to a career in banking. At a time when she was happy and fulfilled as a retail banking area manager, a larger financial institution bought her bank. Her new leadership assigned her to lead a business banking team even though she had no business banking experience, and she didn't want the job. ("What the hell!" I can imagine her saying.)

Her new team included the demoted former leader, an ongoing FBI embezzlement investigation, and an underperforming, inexperienced team. She found herself having to learn her job while coaching her team. Amid this wreckage, Millie built a team with excellent camaraderie and even better performance, despite the negative influence of the disgruntled former team leader. She excelled in her new role, and this assignment changed the trajectory of her career. Moving from retail to commercial banking, she found her work even more personally and financially rewarding.

That opportunity—one she initially did not want—laid the foundation for a very successful career, propelling her to the next job, then the next, and the next. Ultimately, she rose to senior vice president at a major bank.

Remember, great opportunities sometimes come in less-than-pretty packages.

WINGS OF GOLD

hen I graduated from flight school, I earned my wings. With the pomp and circumstance befitting a Navy ceremony, we were awarded our wings at the Naval Aviation Museum. Yes, the same Naval Aviation Museum where I got my first glimpse of "the whale."

This time I walked into the museum proudly and grabbed my seat under the canopy of the Blue Angel diamond formation. Four retired but shiny blue A-4 aircraft hung high above us. It was an impressive sight. Looking up, it immediately took me back to my previous encounter with the Blue Angels. They had "greeted" me the day I arrived in Pensacola nearly a year prior, and here they were "flying high" at my flight school graduation.

Thirteen of us graduated that day, and I was the only woman. At that point, naval aviation had been open to women for just eleven years. At the time, there were fewer than 150 women naval aviators, and we were still new.

One by one we were called forward to receive our wings. The master of ceremonies sounded off, "Ensign Bell graduates with honors—Commandant's List with Distinction." I eagerly leapt forward to receive my Wings of Gold, embracing the fact that my dream had come true. No one could ever take that credential away from me.

Never given too long to celebrate, I still had more training to do before I could join the fleet (the "fleet" is a common term for the operational Navy). It seems aviators never spend much time in any location. Receiving my wings on a Friday, I started Electronic Warfare school the following Monday, spending another twelve weeks in Pensacola. Yes, I received the same training as the men who were headed off to combat squadrons, but I could use my newly acquired skills in a support and training role only. (Do you see a common theme or pattern developing?)

Then it was off to Naval Air Station Key West, Florida, for fleet replacement squadron training in the A-3 aircraft. A fleet replacement squadron (or FRS as we call it) is a squadron dedicated to training aviators in the specific aircraft they are assigned to.

Key West ... how could you not like that place? Warm weather, T-shirts, shorts, flip flops, and flying the skies over the gorgeous Caribbean Sea.

I spent nine months in Key West, learning almost everything there was to know about "the whale" and the systems on board. I flew with combat-trained aviators, practicing aircraft carrier landing patterns (both night and day) to a simulated carrier flight deck—a box marked out on the runway. The training was gritty and good. These aviators helped develop me into a professional aviator.

It was at Naval Air Station Key West that I had my first opportunity to fly to an aircraft carrier for Carrier Qualifications—the process naval aviators go through to get certified to land on an aircraft carrier deck. This was something not many women had the opportunity to do at the time. Only a handful of women flew the C-2 COD (carrier onboard delivery) aircraft to carriers on a regular basis. When I say a handful, I mean one hand only—less than five. They transported mail, parts, and people to and from carriers to keep the logistics supply chain working. These women were only allowed to fly to the carrier during the day; no night operations or overnights allowed. CODs only flew during day ops, with limited exceptions.

We flew from Key West to Naval Air Station Cecil Field near Jacksonville to prepare for CQ (Carrier Qualifications) on board the USS *Saratoga* in the Atlantic. Departing midmorning, we navigated to our assigned position near the carrier and entered into what is called the "Marshall stack"—a strictly determined position far behind the carrier where aircraft go into a holding pattern until cleared to land.

Then I saw it: the USS *Saratoga*.

Aircraft carriers are the largest ships in the Navy. At approximately one thousand feet in length, they have deck space of about 4.5 acres or four football fields. But in the vastness of the Atlantic Ocean, the *Saratoga* looked like a small postage stamp floating alone in the distance.

I swallowed hard. "We're really going to land on that?" I thought.

Once in holding, we waited our turn to land on the carrier. When the call came to push out of the stack, my heart rate began to rise, and my breathing quickened. It was showtime. I was the new navigator flying with a seasoned fleet pilot, LCDR Floyd, or "Pink" as we called him. Leaving the holding pattern, I forgot for a moment to respond to the air traffic controller. Thankfully, Pink covered for me as I composed myself and got back on the radios.

As the carrier came more fully into view, I immediately understood why landing an aircraft on a carrier is one of the hardest things to do *in the world.* One huge, untamable ocean, one small carrier, and one jet aircraft all coming together in what is essentially a crash landing.

While a carrier is the largest ship in the fleet, the eight-hundred-foot long runway pales in comparison to a standard land runway of six thousand to thirteen thousand feet. This is why you don't "flare" the landing on a carrier, touching down and then gradually slowing down. On a carrier landing, you "prang" onto the deck to catch the arresting cable that ultimately stops your forward motion.

We were doing this landing in the daytime with good weather. I could not imagine landing at night in bad weather, with the carrier deck pitching in the ocean and no alternate airfield available. But Pink had done it many times before. He knew exactly what he was doing and was teaching me along the way.

He set the A-3 down on the deck, immediately going to full power in case we missed the "wire" (Navy slang for the arresting cable). The aircraft caught the wire, confirmed by the rapid and abrupt deceleration of the aircraft as we came to a full stop. The aircraft handlers motioned for us to come off the power, then gave us directions to taxi to the catapults. It was the most intense rush I had experienced in my life. The feeling of speed, power, noise, and adrenaline, mixed with anxiety, excitement, and relief all came together in the span of a few seconds.

It all happened so quickly, like a finely orchestrated ballet. Within a few minutes, as the next aircraft prepared to land, we were launched back into the air out over the Atlantic Ocean. Compared to carrier landings, catapult launches are a joy ride. The aircraft is launched from zero to 140 knots (about 160 miles per hour) in just two seconds! With a huge smile emerging under my oxygen mask, I realized I loved that acceleration!

We reentered the landing pattern and prepared to do it all over again. The first landing was breathtaking, but the second was even more exciting. Pink pranged the aircraft onto the deck, we caught the wire and then experienced a complete hydraulic failure. We would not be launching again.

Pink turned to look at me, a smile cracking across his face. "Well, Tinker, I guess you get to spend the night with six thousand men onboard this carrier!" I smiled, too.

We shut down the aircraft, got out, and headed to air operations at the base of the tower. Entering the tower, I took my helmet off, and to the surprise of everyone in the room, they suddenly realized I was a woman. The operations officer took one look at me and began vehemently pointing his finger at me, "You're out of here on the next COD available!"

No woman was going to spend a night on his ship.

Unfortunately, the operations officer got what he wanted. My hopes of an overnight on a carrier were dashed, but I did get two complete carrier landings logged in my logbook. Looking back now, I see that day was a foreshadowing of what was to come. It wouldn't be too many years before women would be present on aircraft carriers, not just overnight, but all the time. Hopefully, I had opened that door just a little bit more.

Soon our squadron made its way back to Key West. After carrier qualifications were completed and the rest of my required flights successfully flown, it was transition time again. I was headed to California and my first official three-year assignment with Tactical Electronic Warfare Squadron Thirty-Four or VAQ-34.

As I drove west on Interstate 10 and passed the exit for Pensacola, memories came flooding back. I had arrived in Pensacola two years prior as a brand-new ensign, not knowing what to expect. Now I was a lieutenant junior grade with a few hundred hours of flight time in my logbook. All the training was behind me—I was a fully qualified aviator.

I had a cross-country drive ahead of me with lots of time for reflection. Long drives will do that. I reminisced about my life—a small-town girl who became a pioneer by going to the Naval Academy. All the ups and downs of the Academy had changed the trajectory of her life. That girl had become a woman, a naval officer, and an aviator … and had landed on an aircraft carrier!

"Heading west" became symbolic for me during that drive. I was setting another course for new frontiers, armed with my proven willingness to take risks, the courage to try new experiences, and the perseverance to follow through.

I was also thrilled that my Academy roommates, Millie and Karen, and I would be stationed within three hours of one another. Millie was making a name for herself at Marine Corps Air Station El Toro, just south of Los Angeles. Karen had earned her surface warfare pin and was a "ship driver" (surface warfare officer) stationed at Naval Base San Diego. And I had earned my aviator wings. Tremendous accomplishments for anyone, let alone three women.

"HEADING WEST" BECAME SYMBOLIC FOR ME DURING THAT DRIVE. I WAS SETTING ANOTHER COURSE FOR NEW FRONTIERS.

Nearly three thousand miles, five days, and lots of junk food later, I arrived at the Pacific Ocean and let out a sigh of relief and anticipation. I began the last leg of my drive heading north on Hwy 101 through Los Angeles, until I arrived at Naval Air Station, Pt. Mugu, California. My next adventure was beginning.

PUSH ON
DESPITE THE NAYSAYERS

Squadron VAQ-34's mission was to prepare the Navy's aircraft carriers and Carrier Air Wings for deployment. We flew simulated enemy tactics against the carriers, jamming their radars and simulating missile attacks on the ships. Each time a carrier prepared for deployment, we were there. We most often flew out of San Diego for the West Coast–based carriers, and Norfolk, Virginia, and Puerto Rico for the East Coast–based carriers. There were a few trips to Hawaii and Alaska too.

With my goal of attending Test Pilot School front and center in my mind, I immediately set about acquiring the one thousand hours of flight time I needed to be competitive. It helped that my first job at my new squadron was flight schedules officer. As luck would have it, I wrote the flight schedule!

I flew anywhere and anytime they needed me, gaining flight hours and additional qualifications along the way. Weekends were no problem for me. Want someone on a cross-country flight? Ask Barb! One of my favorite pilots, Duck, was working to build his flight time as well, although his focus was on the airlines. We flew together often, taking cross-country flights whenever we could.

Life was good, and I was flying a ton. I had arrived at the squadron with about two hundred flight hours. Two hundred hours eventually turned into eight hundred hours. Soon, I could see one thousand flight hours on the horizon. Just as Lt. Colleen Nevius had advised that fateful night during my senior year at the Academy, I had acquired every qualification I could possibly get: navigator, electronic countermeasures officer, maintenance flight check officer, instructor, and mission commander. And I had told every commanding officer that when the time was right, I wanted to go to Test Pilot School, just as Colleen had directed.

TPS is incredibly competitive. Only a portion of Naval Academy graduates go to flight school, and even fewer, far fewer, go to Test Pilot School. TPS students are selected by the selection board, composed of senior TPS graduates, who review every aspect of your professional record. Only a handful of aviators are selected each year to attend Test Pilot School. From this pool of TPS graduates, most astronauts are selected, and pilot astronauts are required to be TPS graduates.

Two years into my first squadron tour, I meticulously began preparing my application for TPS. I met with my career manager (or detailer as we call them in the Navy) to tell him about my desire to go to Navy Test Pilot School.

"So, what do you want to do for your next tour?" he asked.

"I want to go to Test Pilot School," I announced proudly.

His response shocked me. "Test Pilot School? It's hard to get into Test Pilot School," he said with a dismissive tone. "You have to have a really strong record to go to TPS. Well, like mine," he added, with his chest puffed up proudly.

"Like his?" I grumbled silently. Obviously, he had not taken even a moment to look at my record. Given his attitude, I anticipated his next move. Perhaps he would pat me on the head, add the word "honey," and send me on my way. I moved back a few steps to ensure I was out of reach.

"I am applying to the next selection board," I responded, head up and shoulders back.

He mumbled something wholly unremarkable, signaling our conversation was over. "Whatever!" I imagined him thinking.

While a career manager usually writes the orders for your next job, when a selection board is involved, the selection board determines where you will go. My career manager knew that. I knew it too. It wasn't a pissing contest, though it felt a bit like one.

By this point in my career, I was so used to the naysayers that I was not fazed. Not in the least. "Push on regardless," is a saying that has always stuck with me. I pushed on. I knew that I had an excellent record and an excellent chance for selection. The selection board could tell me no, but not my career manager.

When pursuing your dreams, don't listen to the naysayers. Push on. Don't let anyone tell you no, especially if they are not the one who makes the decision.

WHEN PURSUING YOUR DREAMS, DON'T LISTEN TO THE NAYSAYERS. PUSH ON. DON'T LET ANYONE TELL YOU NO.

Even to this day, I counsel people by saying, "You have a 100 percent chance of not getting selected if you don't apply." Are you concerned about getting that next job that seems to require more qualifications than you currently have? Are you worried that the college or graduate program you have always want to attend will not accept you? If you never apply, your odds of acceptance are zero. Guaranteed. Apply, and your odds of selection increase dramatically. Go ahead, go for it. I promise you won't regret it, even if you don't get the job or the acceptance letter.

Janet Bragg lived her life ignoring the naysayers. As she was a pioneering female Black pilot, her race and gender provided constant challenges. Yet she pressed on and overcame every obstacle she faced.

After already earning a nursing degree, Janet enrolled in the Curtiss Wright Aeronautical School in 1933. Although all the students were Black, the others would not help her because she was a woman in a man's occupation. When she discovered the school owned no airplanes for instruction, she purchased her own plane for $600. At the time, Black pilots were not allowed to fly out of airports used by Whites. Undeterred, she helped form a group of Black pilots that purchased land and built their own airfield. By 1934, she had earned her private pilot's license.

When World War II started, she enrolled at the Tuskegee Black pilot training school to obtain a commercial pilot's license. Once again, she encountered discrimination. After she successfully passed ground school and her flight test, her instructor refused to issue her license despite praising her skills. She eventually received her commercial license in 1943 and became the first Black woman to earn a full commercial pilot's license.[14]

---

14   "Janet Harmon Bragg: Aviator," si.edu, February 23, 2017, https://www.si.edu/newsdesk/snapshot/janet-harmon-bragg-aviator.

Apparently, Janet's father constantly reminded his daughter: "If Jack can do it, Jill can do it." Indeed!

Needless to say, I applied to Navy Test Pilot School. When the selection board responded and selected me as the fifth woman ever to be chosen by the Navy, I was elated! (Years later as a Navy commander, in a full-circle moment, I would run the Test Pilot School selection boards and eventually the Navy NASA selection board.) Completely over the moon, I announced to the entire squadron that I was buying the first round of drinks at the Officer's Club that night. My years of hard work and persistence had paid off!

With orders in hand to Test Pilot School, I jumped in my car (at this point a sweet convertible) and drove across the country yet again. This time I was headed to Naval Air Station Patuxent River, Maryland, to join Navy Test Pilot School Class 95. My next dream was coming true.

FLYING HIGH

Thrilled beyond measure, I reported to Navy Test Pilot School, prepared to enter the biggest challenge of my career. Patuxent River Naval Air Test Center (or "Pax River" as it is known colloquially) was to become my home for the next four years—one year as a student at TPS, then two years flying test aircraft with a test squadron, followed by a year as an instructor at Test Pilot School.

My TPS class was filled with the best of the best—the elite—from the Navy, Marine Corps, and Army aviation. In addition, we also had one Air Force, one Coast Guard, and two international military students. Several of my TPS colleagues went on to become astronauts. As was becoming a signature of my career in the Navy, I was the only woman in my class of thirty-three students. Yet I had become so used to being one of the few women, or the only woman, I barely noticed. Perhaps it is a self-protection mechanism. Had I focused on the fact that I was the only woman, it would have taken energy away from my work. Instead, I stayed focused on what was ahead, sensing that there were more distant horizons yet to be seen.

Among the elite, my gender did not matter. By this time, attitudes about women had shifted. We women had been through multiple testing grounds and proven ourselves time and time again. We had graduated from the Naval Academy. We had graduated from flight school. We had become experienced, top-notch aviators.

There was never a question of whether I was qualified. All of us at TPS had been through a challenging selection process—the same process. Gone were the spurious comments that, as a woman, I had taken a spot from a "more qualified" male. Not only was I fully welcomed and accepted, but I was embraced by my male TPS classmates and my instructors. My classmates saw me as their sister, not as their competition.

Test Pilot School was a game changer for me, and it changed the trajectory of my career. After all my years of struggle, I was realizing my dream and it felt … well, it felt *fabulous*! My sincere hope is that women in other sectors, government and the corporate world, experience what I did—that when we are qualified and experienced, we are fully accepted, and gender no longer matters.

Test Pilot School proved to be the hardest work I had ever done in my life. Half of our day was spent in class, and the other half was spent flying all sorts of aircraft. Classes, test plans, test flights, test reports—there was always something we were working on. But despite the workload, we were like kids in a candy store.

Our "candy" was every type of aircraft you could imagine and then some. We flew everything we could get our hands on—jets, props, helicopters—old and new. The school had Navy T-2s, A-4s, F/A-18s (ooh la-la!), Air Force T-38s, Army H-60 and OH-6 helicopters, Coast Guard HH-64s, a Canadian de Havilland Beaver and an Otter (old "tail draggers") and even a few sailplanes. TPS had other aircraft flown in for us to fly, and sometimes we would go other places to fly.

By the time I finished TPS, I had flown over twenty different types of aircraft. By the conclusion of my Navy career, I flew over thirty-five different types of aircraft. I flew fighters, attack planes, transports, and nearly the entire gamut of military and civilian aircraft. I dedicated six days a week to my work, taking one day off to recover. It was heady, intense, and absolutely amazing!

For our final capstone project, each student was assigned an aircraft they had never flown before. We were required to write a full developmental test plan, test our aircraft, and then write a complete report on that aircraft as if it were under developmental testing. Flying our assigned aircraft, we flew to Army, Air Force, and Navy bases across the country or international military bases at European test centers. Once test flights were complete, we had exactly two weeks to complete a test report that was over one hundred pages long. It was equivalent to writing a master's thesis in only two weeks.

Near the end of TPS, I met with the chief test pilot of the Strike Aircraft Test Squadron, my next assignment. Major Dick Ewers, a Marine Corps test pilot, told me that I would be flying the EA-6B, an electronic warfare aircraft. Since we were all getting qualified in two different types of aircraft, he asked me what I wanted my second aircraft to be.

I thought about it for a few (nano) seconds and said, "The F-14 of course," a huge smile breaking across my face.

These were the days after the blockbuster movie *Top Gun* was released, which featured the F-14 fighter aircraft. It was big, bold, and fast. By this point, it had become habit for me to constantly stretch myself. I had nearly made it through TPS, and now the gold ring was within my grasp.

He looked at me with a corresponding smile and said, "If you think you can hack it, I'll get you a class date!"

Major Ewers knew that a woman had yet to become qualified in the F-14, and I probably wouldn't be welcomed with open arms like I had been in TPS. Four women aviators had gone before me in TPS, but the F-14 program was different. This was a premier combat aircraft, a fighter jet, and a squadron filled with "fighter jocks." Women were not part of the equation.

Knowing that as a TPS Distinguished Graduate I could "hack it," Major Ewers scheduled a class date for me. Off to Master Jet Base Naval Air Station Oceana, in Virginia Beach, Virginia, I went. Proud of myself? You bet! For the first time in my career, I was going to fly a first-rate fighter aircraft.

I clearly remember checking in with the fighter squadron duty officer. "Hi, I'm Lieutenant Bell," I said with barely contained enthusiasm.

The duty officer looked up quizzically from his desk. "You're Lieutenant Bell?"

"Yes, I am," I responded with a big smile. I surmised that Major Ewers had not given the squadron my first name when he secured the class date. They had no idea a woman was coming for training. Nevertheless, I was ready. And graciously, the squadron was accepting of me. Since I wouldn't be flying with them in their squadrons and would fly the F-14 in a test scenario only, I was not a threat to them. But the handwriting was on the wall—women would be coming at some point.

The training was fairly quick—ground school and a few flight simulators. The first woman to get qualified in the back seat of the

F-14, I would go on to have my first F-14 flight back at Pax River, among my test pilot school community. That first flight took me back to my childhood dreams of flying. I could never have imagined that those dreams would have led me to an F-14.

In order to soar in our lives, we need to constantly stretch ourselves, so that it becomes natural to do so. Completing one goal does not always mean we must set another goal, and we should definitely take time to enjoy our accomplishments. But achieving a big goal usually leads to new opportunities never before imagined or contemplated. As you progress in your career, keep watching the horizon for where you can go and what you can do next.

IN ORDER TO SOAR IN OUR LIVES, WE NEED TO CONSTANTLY STRETCH OURSELVES, SO THAT IT BECOMES NATURAL TO DO SO.

Several months later, a test pilot and I were flying an F-14 from Pax River to the Grumman Aircraft test facility on Long Island, New York. As we entered into New York City airspace, arguably the busiest airspace in the world, I was on the radio checking in with air traffic control. The normal procedure was to check in with your aircraft call sign and aircraft altitude, then await any further instructions.

In such busy airspace, there is no time for conversation … except on that day. After I checked in with the air traffic controller, there was a long pause.

"Are you in an F-14?" the controller asked.

I looked outside the cockpit at the fuselage and wings of the F-14 and responded with a gentle laugh in my voice, "Well, I was when I took off."

"But you are a woman." I could hear in his voice that he was perplexed.

"Yes, I know that," I responded with another gentle laugh.

"But how is it that you can fly an F-14?"

Then began a conversation where I explained that women were allowed to fly the F-14 in a test role only.

"Wow!" he responded with a note of admiration and respect. "That's incredible that Naval aviation is opening more to women!"

My pilot (with whom I had a good professional relationship) didn't say anything, but I know he was smiling under his oxygen mask. He was pleased to be flying with me.

I felt exhilarated and a bit tickled at the same time. In just five years I had gone from flying an old A-3 that had been relegated to the grassy back field of the Naval Aviation Museum in Pensacola to flying a frontline fighter aircraft. And I had kicked open another door that many other women would later walk through. We women were making progress, and that progress was being noticed and celebrated.

But we weren't where we wanted to be … yet.

You'll be bothered from time to time by storms, fog, snow.
When you are, think of those who went through it before you,
and say to yourself,
"What they could do, I can do."

—ANTOINE DE SAINT-EXUPÉRY

French writer, poet, and pioneering aviator

FIND YOUR WINGS

Below are some questions to get you thinking about where you are now and where you want to be in the future. My hope is that these thought starters will help you identify your goals and dreams and chart a course to achieve them. Visit www. captainbarbarabell.com to download a free tool to help you create your own "flight plan."

WHO IS WATCHING YOU?

Someone in your sphere of influence sees you as a role model. Do you see yourself as the role model that you are? How do you conduct yourself—at work, on social media, with your friends? Are you respectful to all with whom you come into contact?

ARE YOU ACHIEVING YOUR FULL POTENTIAL?

Have you stalled out or gotten too comfortable in your career? Are you doing just enough to get by, or are you going the extra mile every day? What work do you need to do to reach your dreams and goals?

WHAT GIFTS HAVE YOU OVERLOOKED?

Think back to a time in your life when a situation that you initially perceived as negative turned out to be positive. Do you currently have any "unopened gifts"—opportunities you haven't taken advantage of—that could move you toward your goals?

WHO ARE THE NAYSAYERS IN YOUR LIFE?

Are there people in your life telling you that you can't achieve your goals and dreams? Insulate yourself from their negativity. Push on regardless. Make a conscious choice to be around people who support you and encourage you.

HAVE YOU ACHIEVED YOUR INITIAL GOALS?

If so, what's next? Where will you go from here? Now is the time to set your sights on new dreams and goals.

PART THREE:
EARNING YOUR WINGS

*It was the combination of hard work
and a hand up that allowed me
to become one of the first women
to fly in combat missions and achieve
my American Dream.*

—TAMMY DUCKWORTH

US senator and one of the first Army
women to fly combat missions

SQUARE YOUR SHOULDERS

My journey has never been only about me. It has been about opening the way for others to follow, while recognizing that I stand on the shoulders of those who went before me. I stood on the shoulders of the first women military aviators—the WASP (Women Airforce Service Pilots) who flew in World War II. There are many successful military women today, such as Senator Tammy Duckworth and Lt. Col. (retired) Amy McGrath, who followed those first brave female pioneers.

Each of us stands on the shoulders of all the women in our chosen professions who have come before us, who have blazed a trail. Others have done the hard work, and we must too.

Throughout my career, I learned many deepening skills of leadership and was privileged with many opportunities to lead. In flight school, I learned firsthand that I was a role model. I stood out, as I was the only woman in my naval flight officer class. I was watched. I was critiqued. I embraced the experience, sometimes with grace, sometimes not. My calling to leadership included the privilege to be the example. You have the same opportunity and privilege. Once we have earned our wings and gained experience, it becomes our responsibility to lift the next generation.

At one point in my Navy career, I ran the Navy Test Pilot School selection board and the NASA selection board. Fourteen years prior to that, the Navy Test Pilot School selection board had selected me for Test Pilot School, forever changing the trajectory of my career. Four years after graduating from Test Pilot School, the Navy NASA selection board had medically disqualified me based on a positive tuberculosis test. You win some, you lose some. I always kept pressing forward.

ONCE WE HAVE EARNED OUR WINGS AND GAINED EXPERIENCE, IT BECOMES OUR RESPONSIBILITY TO LIFT THE NEXT GENERATION.

I felt incredibly honored to be running both boards. It was a tremendous opportunity to "peek behind the curtain" to see and participate in the process that selects naval officers for these high-level opportunities. My job was to guide both board members and applicants through the selection process. I recruited selection board members and helped applicants prepare their records for the board.

I smile now when I think of the conversations I had with prospective TPS applicants. I counseled them based on my own insights and the timeless advice I had received from Lt. Colleen Nevius so many years ago. True wisdom stands the test of time. While only a fraction of applicants to these boards would be selected, I viewed it as my responsibility to ensure that applicants had the best opportunity for selection.

While running the boards, I noticed more women were applying to Test Pilot School—one to two per selection board instead of one every other year or so during my time. However, the numbers were still low. Along the way, I tried to recruit and mentor as many women as possible for TPS. One woman in particular comes to mind.

I first met Lisa after I graduated from TPS. She was a high school student considering going to the Naval Academy, and she wondered what Navy life was like for a woman. I remember sharing all of the struggles I faced and ultimately the joy I experienced in the challenge. Her father was a Marine test pilot. She had lived the life of military "brat," so she knew much more than I did at her age about what she was getting into. But I think she needed to meet a woman Naval Academy graduate and naval officer firsthand, in order to see herself in the same role. Lisa did attend the Naval Academy, graduated, and became an aviator. In a very proud moment for me during my tenure with the selection board, we selected her for Test Pilot School. Today she is a captain in the Navy and going stronger than ever.

I delightedly continue to follow Lisa's career, as well as the careers of other women I recruited and mentored over the years. I am filled with wonder when I think about where their now-limitless careers will take them. I like to think that I opened doors for them, and now I see that they are "door openers" in their own right.

The real point of finding your wings and learning to fly is not only to soar in your own life, but also to lift others up and bring them along with you. We must square our shoulders for those women who are coming behind us, so they have a solid base to stand on. We need to seek them out, to support and mentor them, so that they can soar to even greater heights than we have.

PAST, PRESENT ...

t was the fall of 1991. I casually strolled into the restaurant by myself and grabbed a table near the bar. The day before, I had come to Sacramento, California, to fly at Mather Air Force Base and to attend my first Women Military Aviators Conference.[15] A few of my friends were attending, and I was excited to meet more women who were changing military aviation. I oftentimes felt quite lonely being the only woman or one of the only women in my particular position. There were so few women aviators at the time that coming together for a conference was a much-needed "shot in the arm" to help us go about our work in the military.

As I sat looking at the menu, I heard a commotion a few tables away. Two older women, whom I guessed to be in their late seventies

---

15   Women Military Aviators is a nonprofit organization formed in 1978 to promote and preserve for historical, educational, and literary purposes the role of women pilots, navigators, and aircrew in the service of their country during times of war and peace. See https://www.womenmilitaryaviators.com.

or early eighties, were talking wildly, hands flying in the air. Obviously, they were having a good time. "Who are they?" I wondered. Their combination of confidence and exuberance struck me, and suddenly I realized they were likely Women Airforce Service Pilots (WASP), the first women military aviators! Captivated, I immediately went over to their table.

"You must be WASP!" I announced with both glee and admiration.

"Yes, we are!" they said with a smile. "Come join us."

In a nanosecond, I grabbed my things and moved to their table. Excited beyond belief, I was going to meet the women who were the first female military aviation pioneers and who made history flying in World War II. I immediately sensed that I was among my tribe. Had I been in the presence of royalty, I would not have been more thrilled. These women made my career possible.

"I'm Bucky, and this is Mary Ann," the first woman said, extending her welcoming hand to me. "My real name is Faith Richards, but everyone calls me Bucky. It's short for Buckner, my last name when I was flying during the war," Bucky said, overflowing with enthusiastic WASP spirit.

"I'm Barb Bell, but my call sign is Tinker, as in Tinker Bell!" I said with a wink.

I joined in their conversation, my own hands suddenly flying in the air. It's funny how aviators need to use their hands to talk; it seems it's the only way we can fully express ourselves. When I speak to audiences today, I use a lavalier microphone to free up my hands in order to tell my stories.

Bucky was a member of WASP Class 43-W-4, the fourth class of women to join the WASP in 1943. (Maybe there is also a connection in that I was in the fourth class of women to attend the Naval Academy, but I digress.) Bucky regaled us with stories of how Jackie

Cochran, founder and director of the WASP, would call her whenever she wanted to open up a new avenue for the WASP. "She'd send me!" Bucky said with a gleam in her eyes. "I flew everything Jackie asked me to fly. But I didn't get the chance to fly pursuit or fighter aircraft as we call them today. Darn it!"

During her WASP career, Bucky flew sixteen different aircraft, including the BT-13 Valiant, AT-6 Texan, B-26 Marauder, and B-24 Liberator.[16] I could clearly imagine this spunky woman as a twenty-something aviator climbing into some of those enormous bomber aircraft. (Although the WASP could not fly bombers in combat, they could fly them in the United States.)

"We were devastated when they disbanded the WASP," Bucky told me, glancing up at the ceiling as if remembering that painful day. "The government sent us home to 'bake cookies.' Can you imagine that?"

"Yes, I can," I said, remembering the discrimination I had faced. I could empathize with the crushing disappointment the WASP experienced as they were sent home at the end of the war. They were disappointed, but not defeated, as I would discover.

"After the war, the airlines would not hire women to fly, but they hired me as a Link simulator instructor," Bucky continued with pride. In my mind, I pictured the blue, boxy, nearly claustrophobic simulator that was used to teach pilots to fly by instruments in bad weather. Sitting outside the simulator, Bucky instructed the male pilots inside, taking them through different scenarios to ensure they could fly confidently using their instruments.

I thought about how frustrated Bucky must have felt not being able to fly for the airlines but teaching men to do so. The irony was

16   For more on Faith Richards, see http://www.wingsacrossamerica.us/web/obits/richards.htm.

not lost on me as I recognized a similar situation I was facing at the time. After completing my first test squadron tour, I had returned to Navy Test Pilot School as the first woman instructor. As a TPS instructor, I could fly fighter aircraft, but only on a test mission. However, I was qualified to teach men who flew combat aircraft in operational squadrons. Like Bucky, I had the knowledge and the skills, but not the opportunity.

"I learned to fly helicopters later in my life," Bucky said, bringing me back to the conversation. "One day, it must have been in the early seventies, I was teaching a new pilot in the Link simulator, and he told me I wasn't really a pilot because I could not fly helicopters. He really pissed me off," she said with a saltiness in her voice. "So I got my rating in helicopters." Bucky had had her fixed-wing aircraft pilot's license for decades, and when she was in her fifties, she became the seventy-fourth woman in the free world to add a helicopter certification to her license.

WE TALKED FOR HOURS, LAUGHING AND SWAPPING STORIES OF FLYING AIRPLANES AND BEING A WOMAN IN A MAN'S WORLD.

Bucky was an instructor for United Airlines, Braniff Airways, and American Airlines, retiring from American in 1986. A proud member of the International Organization of Women Pilots[17] (also known as The 99s), Bucky let nothing—not even the arthritis that I could see crippling her hands—keep her from moving forward in her life.

As more women joined our group, both WASP and current military aviators, hands were "flying" everywhere. We talked for hours, laughing and swapping

---

17   For more information, see www.ninety-nines.org.

stories of flying airplanes and being a woman in a man's world. These women were remarkable. They told stories of flying huge bomber aircraft, training aircraft, and pursuit (fighter) aircraft. Some of the smaller women talked about needing extra seat padding so they could see over the dashboards in the cockpits. One spoke about taking off her flight jacket and top to get a suntan while flying in an open-cockpit aircraft. Many had ferried aircraft from manufacturing plants to bases all over the country. Some were test pilots, and others towed banners for target practice ... for the men.

The members of WASP talked about their lives after the group disbanded. One woman owned and operated an FBO (a small fixed-base operation at a local airport) while continuing to fly throughout her life. Another woman and her husband flew all over the world collecting snake venom to make antivenom. Another had been an instructor pilot in Florida and California, then a bush pilot in Alaska delivering JCPenney catalogues all over the state.

Although the conversation occasionally dipped into what we couldn't do, we focused far more on what we could do and the many adventures we had experienced in our lives. The bartender told me later he had never experienced such energy in the place. I wasn't surprised.

Later on, during the conference, we took a bus trip to a local tourist site. As I walked to the bus, I noticed a white Corvette with a specialized license plate emblazoned with "WASP" parked in a reserved handicapped spot. I had to know which WASP owned that beauty of a sports car. I boarded the bus and yelled out, "Hey, who owns that white Corvette in the handicapped spot?"

A woman who had pulled herself onto the bus using her cane returned my volley, "It's mine; so what?"

"Well, I want to be just like you when I grow up!" I smiled back. To this day, I still want to be like the WASP.

That weekend was joyous. I met so many women aviators, and I was reminded that I was not alone and got the boost I needed. It felt like a trifecta win for sure! It was even more special because Bucky and I developed a profound connection that weekend, which sustained me for years to come. When I think of her now, I feel a deep sense of strength well up inside me.

The conference served as yet another turning point for me. I had come to personally know the women who were our country's first female military aviators. From this point forward, I was not only walking in their footsteps, but also laying a path for the women military aviators to come.

... AND FUTURE

As women began to graduate from the Naval Academy in the eighties, the Naval Service was forced to change to accommodate the highly qualified women the Academy was producing. No longer would these women accept traditional administrative jobs in the Navy and Marine Corps. As a result, the service began opening up more jobs and in greater numbers to these newly commissioned women officers in areas such as naval aviation and naval surface warfare. As these women continued to succeed and progress in their naval careers, their presence forced additional changes in the service.

Soon after the first Gulf War ended in 1991, the political debate began about what combat roles women aviators could and should hold. Up until this point, women had flown in the Gulf War, but only in support roles because of the combat exclusion laws. The reality, however, was that *women were in combat*, just not recognized as combat aviators. They flew support aircraft carrying supplies to the front lines, but their aircraft could not be armed. Essentially, women could be shot at, but could not shoot back. It was time for change.

As an instructor at Navy Test Pilot School, I worked for a fantastic Navy department head, Commander Dave Kennedy, and an exceptional Marine Corps commanding officer, Lt. Col. Bob Price. Both of these leaders supported my work and, more broadly, helped expand the roles of women in military aviation. Lt. Col. Price wrote on my FITREP (annual performance evaluation or fitness report), "I would serve with her in combat." This was not something to be taken lightly, as he had documented in writing his position on women flyers.

As the debate grew, I went to Washington, DC, armed with Lt. Col. Price's documented support. I joined with my women aviator's network, Women Military Aviators (WMA), and we began our work to repeal the combat exclusion laws. Captain Rosemary Mariner, the first woman to qualify as a Navy jet pilot, spearheaded our charge. Along with other women military aviators, both active duty and reserve, we in WMA joined forces with the WASP, the National Organization of Women (NOW), and the Women's Research Education Institute (WREI).

Together, we traversed the halls of Congress and educated those in Washington on the combat aviation roles women were qualified to fill. We attended strategy meetings, met with our congresswomen and congressmen, were interviewed on television and wrote articles for the *Washington Post*. We showed them what real women military aviators looked like and that we had the skills, confidence, and mettle to fly combat aircraft.

One of the congressmen I had the privilege of speaking with was the senator who had appointed me to the Naval Academy. He welcomed us into his office, and as we spoke, I felt my passion welling up within me and said, "You appointed me to the United States Naval Academy in 1979. It is now time that you give me equal opportunity in the Navy, sir."

I do not know that he remembers that conversation. However, I will remember it for the rest of my life. There I was in the halls of Congress, the girl from a small town in Michigan, now a naval officer, speaking my truth. I had come a long way. *We* had come a long way.

That senator listened. Many other congresswomen and congressmen listened as well. In 1993, we celebrated as the combat exclusion laws were repealed, allowing women to fly combat aircraft and to serve

WE SHOWED THEM WHAT REAL WOMEN MILITARY AVIATORS LOOKED LIKE AND THAT WE HAD THE SKILLS, CONFIDENCE, AND METTLE TO FLY COMBAT AIRCRAFT.

on combatant ships. Today, women in the military fly everything men fly, and they are increasingly more visible. Women Naval Academy graduates have risen to the ranks of captain, colonel, admiral, and general. Admiral Michelle Howard (USNA class of 1982) became the first woman to serve as a four-star admiral, held the second-highest position in the Navy as vice chief of naval operations, and served as the commander of Naval Forces Europe.

We see the trickle-down effect in areas previously dominated by men. Women are running Fortune 500 companies—Fortune 50 companies, in fact. Women are leading universities. Women are astronauts. There is even greater progress in politics. Women are taking control of more seats in Congress and wielding tremendous power. (Several of them are Naval Academy graduates who were also aviators.)

As of the writing of this book, women make up over a quarter of the 117th Congress, the highest percentage in US history and a significant increase from just ten years ago. Women have achieved the roles of speaker of the house and secretary of state, and now Kamala Harris serves as vice president of the United States. Globally, 22 out of 193 countries have a female head of state or government. Truly, women are changing the world.

Change takes time, but change is happening. It is true that not all of us may be able to change the world, but each and every one of us can change our piece of it. Start by changing what is in your sphere of influence. Get involved. Make your presence known. Become an active voice for the change you want to see.

STEP OUT ON FAITH

My time on Capitol Hill reinforced the importance of putting myself "out there." As I continued to rise through the ranks in the Navy, my influence increased, and my visibility as a role model grew exponentially.

Although we joyously celebrated the repeal of the combat exclusion laws, I was not allowed to go to a combat squadron. I had been promoted to lieutenant commander (LCDR) by this point, and I was deemed by the Navy to be "too senior" to transfer into a fighter squadron. I had to once again change my flight plan. Certainly, I was disappointed. But at the same time, I was proud that what I had accomplished in the Navy had helped change our lawmakers' minds.

Sometimes we open doors for ourselves, and sometimes we open doors for others.

The alternate pathway for me was to go more deeply into research, development, test and evaluation. I transferred into the aerospace engineering duty officer community, where I worked in program and project management and what I call "the business side of the Navy." There is a huge support system that keeps our Navy's ships, aircraft, submarines, and associated equipment up and running.

SOMETIMES WE OPEN DOORS FOR OURSELVES, AND SOMETIMES WE OPEN DOORS FOR OTHERS.

By late summer of 1992 I received orders to attend Naval Postgraduate School to get my master of science degree in astronautical (or space systems) engineering. For obvious reasons, there are not many naval installations in the middle of the country. So, with a calculator and a stash of mechanical pencils in hand, I was off once again to California, this time to Monterey.

With its shining waters and raw, rocky coastline, Monterey was exquisite. School was demanding, but by this point in my career, I knew how to manage challenges and still have time for family, friends, and myself. I vowed that never again would I work as hard as I did in Test Pilot School, where I worked six days a week with little time for anything else. I had proven myself many times over prior to getting to graduate school. In Monterey, I was able to compartmentalize and treated school as an eight-to-five job. I worked hard during the day and studying during free periods, but when the day was over, school was done.

After school, I volunteered with the Boys and Girls Club, learned to surf and kayak, and enjoyed some down time for myself. Allowing space in your life opens you to opportunities. It was in Monterey that I met Andy, the Navy helicopter pilot who would become my husband.

After completing my master's degree, I received orders to move once again across the country to Washington, DC. This time, my new husband, Andy, came with me. By this point in my life, I had moved across the country so many times, it seemed I knew the highways by heart. Now, I was on my way to the National Reconnaissance Office to work on their satellite programs. I cannot get into the specifics of my work, but I became the integration and test lead for a major satellite program.

As my three-year tour at the National Reconnaissance Office came to a close, I received a call from my favorite mentor from Test Pilot School, Captain Steve "Smiley" Enewold (he ultimately retired as a two-star admiral). Smiley and I shared a special connection. Years later, he would be the guest speaker at my retirement, and I would serve as master of ceremonies for his.

I still vividly remember that phone conversation. "Hey, Barb, I'd like you to come work for me," he said in his warm, smiling voice. His call sign was Smiley, and it fit his personality perfectly.

Without even knowing what the job entailed, I immediately responded, "Yes!" When you are lucky enough to have a mentor like Smiley offer you a job or opportunity, jump on it! Step out on faith. The details can be worked out later.

Leaving Washington, DC, I went back to Patuxent River, Maryland, to work in the EA-6B Prowler aircraft program office at Naval Air Systems Command. The Prowler is the electronic warfare aircraft I had flown after Test Pilot School during my test tour. The program office and Naval Air Systems Command are responsible for providing full life-cycle support for naval aviation, from procurement of new aircraft and associated systems to aircraft upgrades and logistics.

While working for Smiley, I was promoted to commander and selected for my first command.[18] I know what you are thinking—back to California. Not this time. This time, Andy and I moved halfway around the world for my job as commander, Defense Contract Management Command Australia, located in Melbourne, Australia.

It was an honor to be the first woman to hold command in Australia and in the international division of the Defense Contract Management Agency. I was so used to being "the first woman in the job," I often forgot that having a woman commander was a new experience for many people that I worked with. Expectations were unknown and different.

Perhaps not surprisingly, the men who worked *for* me generally had no issue with my being a woman. Women were much more common in the Navy by this time, and these men had come up through the ranks with many highly qualified women.

But there were a few challenges with men above me at the upper levels. I was a woman *and* a highly prepared, experienced, and credentialed naval officer. I think there were times that my boss in Japan did not know what to do with me. It was rocky at first, but eventually we worked things out.

Millie, my Academy roommate, once told me, "I choose to not let being a female in a male-dominated world be *my* problem; I let it be *their* problem." Good advice!

I have found throughout my career that graciousness and a warm smile go a long way when others are wary of you because you are

---

18   A command in the Navy is an individual unit (a ship, a squadron, an air wing, a shore organization, etc.) that is led by an officer who is entrusted with the singular authority, responsibility, accountability, and expertise to accomplish the mission. In accordance with Navy regulations, "You accept the extraordinary responsibility of command with full regard for the consequences."

different. I consciously extended myself into my new community, and the Australians in my command and in the external community responded with an exceptional welcome. I learned to say, "She'll be right, mate" and "No worries."

Before long, I became quite a novelty in Melbourne, and this is where my speaking career took off. Prior to leaving for Australia, I had completed a public speaking course to further hone my speaking skills, as I knew that the best leaders are competent and inspiring speakers. It paid off.

First, the wives of the male officers at the Naval and Military Club invited me to be their luncheon speaker. Then, the men followed suit, asking me to their next event. Through their networks, one speaking engagement led to another, then another and another—the snowball effect, as they say. I was invited to speak at the Defense Force Academy in Canberra (Australia's capital) and at clubs and schools across the state of Victoria. I had not been intent on developing a speaking career; it happened organically. But the more I shared my story with others, the more I realized I had something important to say.

Too often we think we have to have it all figured out before we head down a new path or begin a new opportunity. I had become quite adept at risk taking by this point. I came to relish it in fact. I had become comfortable stepping out on faith and trusting that something positive would come from the risks and opportunities I took.

Taking on my first command was certainly new ground for me. I did not know everything that would be expected of me, but no leader does. As you become more senior in your leadership, let go of the notion that you have to know everything. As your leadership responsibilities grow and become increasingly more complex, become comfortable being more of a generalist. Rely on those who work for you as the specialists and lead them in the direction you want them to go.

That first command in Australia led to a second career as a burgeoning speaker. Today, I am regularly asked to speak at events from graduation commencements and university club luncheons to Veterans Administration events, various women's and men's professional groups, and of course, schools. I appreciate the opportunities to share my story and encourage others to stand out when they don't fit in.

It only takes one step or one event to snowball into something truly incredible. Step out on faith. Take that first step, and you will be amazed with the opportunities that will unfold. I know I have.

DON'T CLIP
YOUR OWN WINGS

Word got out across Melbourne that this Navy woman was willing to tell her story. One day I received a call inviting me to speak at the mother-daughter dinner at the Lyceum Club, a university women's club founded in 1912. The format of the evening was particularly appealing, as I would speak first, then we would eat dinner, leaving lots of time for engaging conversation.

"Answering the Call: One Naval Officer's Perspective," the title of my speech, served as an invitation to audience members to consider responding to their life's calling. As I finished speaking, the room was buzzing. I knew I had hit a nerve. After openly sharing my personal story, others began telling theirs. Mothers turned to their daughters and to one another, sharing what they had been called to do in their lives.

One young woman walked straight over to me. Louise, a doe-eyed nineteen-year-old, introduced herself and thanked me for my talk. I will always remember her next words: "Now I know what I want to do with my life!"

I was stunned. In that moment, the reason that I volunteered so much of my time speaking to others became crystal clear: I share my story so that I might influence the lives of others, inspiring young women (and men) to see opportunity and help launch their lives.

Louise went on to explain, "I want to fly, but I don't know how to go about it." As we continued our conversation, her enthusiasm washed over me. I offered her my business card and asked her to call. We could discuss her future and figure out how she might take the next step.

Louise called my office the next day. She remembered something I had shared with the audience the night before—when you are offered an opportunity, take it! "There will be willing mentors along your path," I'd said to the group. "They will open doors for you, but through those doors only *you* can walk."

Louise and I soon met for coffee and thus began a beautiful mentoring relationship. We spoke about two distinct paths to becoming a pilot: military and civilian. I gave Louise the assignment to check out both, and she ultimately determined that civil flight training would fit her best. She enrolled in a three-year flight program at a local university.

Several months into flight training, Louise called me with concern in her voice. "I don't think I'll ever get this." She was having trouble understanding the engineering, math, and physics behind the dynamics of flight. I offered to tutor her after work, and together we developed her understanding of the fundamentals of flight. With my encouragement, she pushed forward.

Nearly a year into her program, Louise called again. Sheepishly she told me, "I'm moving to be near my boyfriend."

"Will you keep flying?" I asked, already sensing the answer.

"No, but I'll get back to it someday," Louise said.

"Someday?" I responded angrily.

Yes, I was annoyed that I would lose the investment of time I had made in Louise, but I was upset that she would give up her dream. I get infuriated when women "clip their own wings." Sometimes we clip our own wings because we do not believe in ourselves. We do not trust that we have the skills or experience to achieve what we want to achieve. So we sell ourselves short, often before we even get started.

Sometimes we clip our own wings by not making our dreams and goals a priority. I have seen young women put their lives on the back burner for a relationship or even just the *potential* of a relationship. I'm not sure why. Perhaps it is the social conditioning that women should put others before themselves. Of course, many women and men will have to make compromises as they work to balance family and career. But no one should compromise at any time to the point that they abandon their dreams and goals. There is always a way to keep moving forward toward your dreams.

SOMETIMES WE CLIP OUR OWN WINGS BY NOT MAKING OUR DREAMS AND GOALS A PRIORITY.

In my mind, the boyfriend could wait. Louise needed to get her education. I jumped right in with, I admit, somewhat of a guilt trip. "Louise, I have invested heavily in you. *You owe me* one more year in flight training!"

There was silence on the other end of the phone.

"*One. More. Year!*" I demanded. I knew Louise was in a three-year program, and my demand would not get her to the end. My hope was that if she agreed to an interim milestone and then reached it, she would finish the entire three-year course.

Shaken by my response, Louise reconsidered. Her dream, though clouded by her relationship, was still alive. She put the move on hold, stayed with her program, and ultimately finished and earned her pilot's license. Louise has since told me she was truly glad I had given her the push she needed.

I cannot stress enough the importance of finding a mentor. Man or woman, it doesn't really matter. However, if women can find other women as mentors and role models, that is even better. Women share in a different way than men. They collaborate more and share more of the lived experience of managing family and work life. Millie has the same perspective: "My advice to women today is to seek advice and mentorship from other women senior in your field, your church, or even a professional female in another field."

Plans and dreams can quickly get derailed if we let them. It is all too easy to let "life" get in the way. We tell ourselves we will do "it" later, never to pick "it" up again. This is why an accountability partner or mentor is crucial. They help us see when we are limiting ourselves and clipping our own wings. They keep our dream in front of us, push us, and remind us to keep flying when we want to ground ourselves.

INSPIRE ONE ANOTHER

Melbourne had captured my heart, but after two years, it was time to leave Australia. I promised Louise I would stay in touch. We packed up once again and said a tearful goodbye to our many Aussie friends. My next duty station was in Millington, Tennessee (near Memphis), at the Navy Personnel Command, where I would become a detailer or career manager. And yes, I was the first woman in that job. I was going to do things differently and relationally. Many people are afraid of their detailer, but I was not going to be feared.

Do you remember the career manager who many years prior suggested my record was not strong enough to get me into Test Pilot School? As I began my new assignment, I vowed never to discourage, only to encourage, my constituents. I loved my work. The daily personal interaction I had with the officers in my career field energized me. One-on-one coaching is what I call it today. Sometimes I met with my constituents in person, but more often I was on my phone headset, counseling, coaching, and assigning orders to my members. I listened deeply to their stories, helping them make trade-offs among personal desires, professional career progression, and, of course, the needs of the Navy.

While stationed in Millington, I decided to take an adult education class on life coaching at the University of Memphis. As I sat waiting for class to start on the first night, my eyes scanned the room. I quickly noticed an elegant blonde woman two seats away. Studying her for a moment, I noticed her unique ring—a pair of WASP wings wrapped around her finger. As the woman appeared to be about my age, I wondered how she had acquired them.

At the break, I leaned over to introduce myself. "Hi, I'm Barb. Aren't those WASP wings?" I asked, pointing to her finger. "And how is it you have them?"

"Hi, I'm SaraLyn. Yes! They are my grandmother's," she said with a smile spreading across her face. "How did you know?"

"I'm a big fan of the WASP. They are the women I look up to. I'm an aviator myself."

SaraLyn Archibald, granddaughter of WASP Betty Archibald of class 43 W-3 (the one prior to Bucky's), and I began an amazing friendship that night. The more we got to know each other, the more we felt that the WASP spirit is part of who we are. SaraLyn has real WASP DNA; I have it by association. Betty passed to SaraLyn the tenacity and persistence she developed as a WASP. SaraLyn soars in her life too—not as an aviator, but as an award-winning high school drama teacher.

As we continued to talk, SaraLyn's eyes suddenly lit up. "You've got to meet my grandmother!" she exclaimed.

I couldn't imagine anything better. Bucky had recently passed away, and I longed for another personal connection to the WASP. A few months later, I headed to the Tunica Museum in Tunica, Mississippi, where Betty Archibald had been invited to be the guest speaker for a featured WASP exhibit.

Dressed in my khakis and flight jacket, I walked into the museum and spied Betty in the distance—a powerhouse in a very small package. I think Betty was all of five feet tall. I towered above her at five feet, nine inches. SaraLyn would tell me later that Betty was exactly five feet, two and a half inches when she joined the WASP, just tall enough to meet the minimum height requirement. When Betty became a WASP, she weighed ninety-eight pounds and would be required to carry one hundred pounds of gear including her parachute. Now that was one strong woman!

Betty flew everything she could get her hands on, including pursuit or fighter aircraft. After the WASP disbanded, she became an air traffic controller at Meigs Field in Chicago and later in Indianapolis. She was the first female air traffic controller at both airfields. One of my favorite stories about Betty is that she did not drive to work. She flew her airplane to work, parking it at the base of the air traffic control tower! The men didn't always know what to make of this woman. I understood that sentiment completely.

Betty and I connected immediately. A photographer from the local newspaper captured that connection and published it in the Tunica newspaper. That picture is one of my favorite photographs. Betty is in *her* version of a WASP uniform (she gets creative with uniforms). It is a moment frozen in time I will never forget. As I looked into her eyes, I saw the past—one of the women who made my life's work possible. And as she looked at me, I believe she saw her legacy.

During her presentation, Betty spoke in typical air traffic controller style, what I call "burst transmissions" of information—quick, staccato, and to the point. In less than ten minutes, she was done. "Well, that's all I have to say. Barb is far more interesting," she said, turning to look directly at me. "Why don't you come up here and tell your story?"

I had been put on the spot. SaraLyn just smiled. With no notes or time to prepare, I walked to the front of the room, composed myself for a few seconds, then stood next to Betty and told my story as a continuation of hers.

Betty is gone now, but I keep that deep connection to the WASP through SaraLyn, one of my dearest friends. I keep the picture on the following page, and the one of Betty and me, prominently displayed in my home. They serve as reminders that when we are open to connecting with others, role models in particular, we find ourselves buoyed by their experience and pulled forward in our own lives.

I encourage you to not only seek out women role models but to also see yourself as a role model and mentor. In a recent conversation with a female colleague, we spoke about the fact that during our mostly male-dominated careers (she in engineering, I in naval aviation), we had mentors, but we had few, if any, role models. "We are the role models now," she said to me, and she was right.

Now, as an educator, I know that girls and young women must be exposed to role models. They must be able to see themselves in the future majors they select in college and in the careers that may follow. They need to "see it to be it," as so many mentors say.

I ENCOURAGE YOU TO NOT ONLY SEEK OUT WOMEN ROLE MODELS BUT TO ALSO SEE YOURSELF AS A ROLE MODEL AND MENTOR.

When I was the director of the Center for STEM Education for Girls in Nashville, Tennessee, we held a STEM Summer Institute each year. I brought in a diverse group of younger women in STEM to speak to the girls about their careers. We had an electrical engineer turned pastor, a professor of civil and architectural engineering, a chemical engineer who is now an international security policy specialist, an astrophysicist who now studies museum science, and a Vanderbilt University biomedical engineering PhD candidate. All in their twenties and early thirties, these women were diverse in experience, background, race, and ethnicity. What they had in common was their dedication to developing the next generation.

As the girls in the institute listened to the women tell their personal stories of challenge and accomplishment, I watched both the speakers and the audience. The speakers could see themselves as they had been just several years prior—on the cusp of going to college, seeking to forge a path forward, embracing the unknown. And the girls were beginning to see themselves in their own futures, in work and in lives never before imagined.

The girls were inspired, and so were the speakers.

One of our speakers wrote to me afterward. "Visiting your camp, meeting your girls, and seeing so much promise for our future was a huge source of inspiration for me. My interaction with them, particularly the bright young student I had a chance to pull aside at the end, really touched my heart."

That's how the cycle works. We seek to inspire others and in doing so, we become inspired. We need more women inspiring other women—older to younger, as well as younger to older. Whenever I interact with the young women of the next generation, my eyes light up. My heart, too, is filled. And I'm willing to bet yours will be too.

TIME TO GO ASHORE

y time in Memphis was a brief eighteen months, and before I knew it, I was headed back to Patuxent River, Maryland. Two-star admiral and fighter pilot Rear Admiral Gib Godwin had called me one day in Memphis. Admiral Godwin had taken notice of me several years prior when I was working for Smiley. "It's time you come back here!" he said in his gravelly Texas accent, and then he asked me to be his chief of staff. His call felt like a hand up to the next opportunity. Indeed it was.

While working in Patuxent River, Andy and I joyously adopted our son, David, and began life as a family of three. He was a beautiful four-year-old with high energy, jet back hair, and soulful eyes. I had waited years to become a mother, and now my wish had finally come true.

As chief of staff, I was in a key position of responsibility and visibility for the next command selection board. That was the admiral's hand up to me—the opportunity for the best positioning for selection for command. During my time as chief of staff, I was promoted to captain, and then I was selected for my second command.

I was thrilled, as it was a "major command" in the program management area and exactly what I wanted. Thank you, Admiral Godwin! My official title was "Program Manager for Air Traffic Control and Combat Identification Systems." (What a mouthful!) I was responsible for a portfolio of high-impact programs for the Department of the Navy and the Department of Defense. And I was the first woman aviator selected for such a position across the Department of the Navy.

I oversaw six hundred people, a $400 million annual budget, and a new-technology $1.2 billion air traffic control program. It felt like an honor, a mountain, and a jigsaw puzzle combined. This command was responsible for all air traffic control systems for Navy and Marine Corps aviators across the globe, on land and onboard ships, twenty-four hours a day, seven days a week. It was a CEO-equivalent position of a very large business, except with lives at stake. It was high visibility and high pressure. But twenty-five years into my naval career, I was up for the task.

The command was struggling when I arrived. With focus on "sexier" program offices such as the F/A-18 or Joint Strike Fighter programs, this command had been pushed aside for years and was nearly invisible within the larger Naval Air Systems Command. One of the reasons I was selected was because of the visibility I could bring to the organization. My task was to turn things around. I saw it as an opportunity—a diamond in the rough.

My strategy was to engage the entire, fragmented command as a team. From day one, I referred to every individual as a team member and to the group as a team. I knew I alone could not fix the situation;

only my team could do so. I would provide the vision, and they would do the heavy lifting. Just as Smiley had taught me, I delegated as much as possible and empowered my team leads.

I introduced my concept of values-based leadership that I had used in my previous command. I had developed it throughout my career, and it became the framework for my leadership. Today, I advise all leaders to write down their concepts of leadership and to share them within their organizations.

I led by my personal values statement, which I published, and challenged my team members to hold me accountable to those values. I showed them daily that my values of teamwork, truth, honesty, and respect could become the values of the organization.

Soon, we began to think and act like a team. Together we turned around our struggling programs and set them on a course to success. Our organization became known for excellence. It was my most significant leadership accomplishment, and I could not have been prouder. It was the culmination of all the years of investments that had been made in me, and all that I had made in others.

One day I was called to report to the admiral's office. No explanation was offered. A bit confused to say the least, I began thinking, "Will this be a counseling session or a new job offer or what?" I reported as directed and was greeted by Vice Admiral Venlet, the commander of Naval Air Systems Command (NAVAIR), and his deputy, Rear Admiral Smiley Enewold. Quizzically I looked at them, wondering what was coming next. They broke into huge smiles, then ushered me into the conference room. There before me was my entire leadership team, along with a few of my favorite colleagues.

The admirals spoke together, "Captain Bell, you have been awarded the T. Michael Fish Award for leadership and quality of work life. Your team submitted your name for this award, and across our twenty-two-thousand-member NAVAIR organization, you have been selected. Congratulations!"

Overcome with emotion and humbled by what I saw, I was speechless. Tears still come to my eyes as I remember the moment. My team had accepted my challenge and completely embraced our mission. My values had become the values of the organization. The quality of their work multiplied, and most importantly, their work lives were enriched by becoming a single team. It was perhaps the proudest moment of my career. Remember what I said about lifting others up and bringing them with you? There is no greater sense of fulfillment.

A few months later, after coming down from the euphoria of receiving the award, I began to do some serious reflecting on my future. My work was exhilarating but also exhausting. Being a Navy program manager comes with a great deal of stress. It takes a lot of emotional, mental, and physical effort to turn around a struggling organization. In addition, the frequent two-to-three-hour drives to and from the Pentagon to defend our budgets and push our programs forward was taking a toll. My team was doing exceptional work. Knowing that our program office, programs, and team were on solid footing, I recognized that I had accomplished all that I had set out to do. It was time for someone else to take over.

But what to do next?

I knew I was competitive for flag officer, but becoming a flag officer, although incredible, would mean far less flexibility and longer work hours. The runway for continued professional success was ahead of me, but also the opportunity for an off ramp. I began to feel the tug to retire. I could feel it as if it were tapping at my shoulder. Time to "go ashore" as they say in the Navy.

I also wanted more flexibility in my life and to spend more time with my family. Our family of three was soon to expand to four, as we were in the process of adopting our daughter, Kim Anh. You can be a very successful woman—even in the military—and still have a family. Career and family have never been either/or propositions for men and shouldn't be for women either. Sometimes that is the perception, but it doesn't need to be.

Work-life balance is always a challenge. When I counsel women (and men), I tell them that you can have it all, but not all at the same time. There are always trade-offs. We have to

CAREER AND FAMILY HAVE NEVER BEEN EITHER/OR PROPOSITIONS FOR MEN AND SHOULDN'T BE FOR WOMEN EITHER.

be honest with ourselves as to the trades we are willing to make. For me, the trade-offs weren't so obvious anymore. Closing in on twenty-eight-plus years in the Navy, I was ready for a change. And retiring as a Navy captain is no small thing.

One glorious fall day, amid much pomp and circumstance as is fitting for a Navy Change of Command and Retirement, Admiral Steve *Smiley* Enewold delivered his address as my retiring officer. After Smiley stepped back from the podium, I stepped forward with a flight bag full of mixed emotions to offer my last words.

I spoke about my wondrous journey from a small town to the Naval Academy to a career in the Navy, thanking all who had helped me along the way. Much had changed in the Navy during my career, and I had accomplished more than I had ever imagined. I had flown more than 1,600 hours in thirty-five different types of aircraft. I had gone where few women, and many times no woman, had ever gone before. I had grown tremendously both personally and professionally, learning to welcome new challenges and lean into opportunities. I had traveled the world, becoming more sensitive to cultures other than my own. And I had developed a strong, confident voice which I shared willingly with others.

My whole family was in attendance and nodded their support as I spoke. My parents, who had expected each of us to go to college, had no idea that I would turn that expectation into a stunning Naval career. (Frankly, neither did I.) My brother Dan, who had initially discouraged me from going to the Naval Academy, became a huge supporter, as did my brother Jim. In addition to our bond as siblings, we shared the bond of military service. They both were Air Force officers. Dan got out of the Air Force after his initial five-year commitment and went into the private sector, but Jim, also working in industry, was still in the Air Force Reserves.

My Academy roommates Millie and Karen were there too, along with several of my Naval Academy and Test Pilot School classmates. So many had witnessed and participated in my Naval career. They were there to help me mark both an ending and a new beginning.

Finally, with a tinge of sadness in my voice and a sense of uncertainty about my future, I read aloud my official orders to retire. "When directed by reporting senior, detach from current duty ... and proceed to home of selection." My heart skipped a few beats. Minutes later I rendered my final salute. I was going ashore. As difficult as it was, as I looked out on the face of my young son, I knew it was the right decision.

I think the Naval Service does it right. We must celebrate our accomplishments and our transitions, both beginnings and endings. Transitions are part of a full life. Endings are often bittersweet. Once we complete a phase of life, we cannot go back. Life moves us forward ... on to the next adventure. And my life's work was hardly complete. It was only changing course.

SEEING OPPORTUNITY

Wanting to try something new, we moved to Hood River, Oregon, a niche of high tech near Portland. I wanted my children to grow up in a small town where kids walk to school and people value community connections. I began consulting part time in the aerospace sector, working for companies like Boeing and Insitu. They valued my program management experience and wanted my insights into how to do business with the Navy, along with access to my Navy connections. I often walked only five blocks down the road to work. Feeling free, I never wore a hat or uniform, and sometimes I believe I even skipped to work.

One day at home, I unexpectedly received a large yellow envelope in the mail. Although there was no return address, the package had a cancelled stamp from Australia. I quickly tore open the envelope. Inside was a newspaper with a yellow sticky note at the margin, luring me to an inside page. There was a picture of a smiling Louise, standing next to her aircraft in a full-page spread! Not only had Louise become a pilot, but a commercial pilot flying the Australian outback. She had started her own flying business, Central Eagle Aviation, providing custom charters and tourist flights.

The article, "Thrilled to Fly the Wild Route,"[19] told of Louise's challenges in becoming a commercial pilot. As one of only two women in her class of thirty-five, she struggled with being a minority in a male-dominated field. (Even today in the United States, women represent less than 7 percent of commercial pilots.[20] Across the globe, the numbers vary, yet women remain in the minority.)

Although there was no note from Louise, the article conveyed her sentiments. In the article, she spoke of how the academics of flying were difficult for her and how she was willing to ask for help. She also told of my willingness to mentor her because I had been mentored. That is how life works, or should work anyway. Usually, a mentor has been previously mentored by someone else and then pays it forward to others. Louise had found her strength by holding onto her dream. I beamed with pride. Nothing fills me up more than seeing someone I have mentored find success.

A few months prior to my fiftieth birthday, a friend asked how I was going to celebrate. I had not planned on anything in particular. She encouraged me to rethink my plans, offering that turning fifty is a life event to be celebrated. I asked myself, "If I could do anything, what would I do?" I knew immediately. I would fly the Australian outback with Louise!

---

19 *Centralian Advocate*, Alice Springs, Friday, January 8, 2009, 4–5.

20 "Current Statistics of Women in Aviation Careers in U.S.," Women in Aviation International 2019, https://www.wai.org/resources/waistats; and "2018 Active Civil Airmen Statistics," Federal Aviation Administration, https://www.faa.gov/data_research/aviation_data_statistics/civil_airmen_statistics/.

Filled with excitement, I contacted Louise and told her of my idea to visit and fly with her. She was thrilled at the thought. "I won't be able to fly with you, though," she said. "I'm pregnant with twins."

My heart sank momentarily before I was filled with excitement for her. This young woman had become a pilot, a business owner, a wife, and now a soon-to-be mother. I knew Louise had potential when I first met her as a nineteen-year-old, and now, years later, she was realizing it.

It was settled. I would celebrate my fiftieth birthday with Louise at Pandie Station, a 1.6-million-acre cattle station that her husband managed just outside the quintessential outback town of Birdsville. Although I could not fly with Louise, I would get to fly the outback with her Central Eagle Aviation pilots.

Several months later, I boarded the fifteen-hour Qantas flight from Los Angeles to Sydney. I had plenty of time to parse out my feelings during those long flights. I was elated that I was marking this milestone birthday in such an unusual way and that I would be able to reconnect with Louise. And I was amazed and a bit saddened that my Navy career was behind me, although still bearing fruit. I had mentored many along the way, and Louise was the shining example of why I invested in others.

From Sydney I flew to Melbourne, and from there, I took a smaller plane to Alice Springs, the nearly desolate center of Australia. In Alice Springs, I located the small FBO (fixed based operation—pilot speak for aviation businesses at local airports) and began looking for Central Eagle Aviation's Cessna 210 as Louise had indicated. Suddenly I heard, "Good day, Barb!" and saw two pilots waving me over to the tarmac.

Soon we were airborne. As we bumped along for another couple of hours across the dusty sands of the Simpson desert to Birdsville (population 120), I was stunned by the sheer enormity of the outback. The continent of Australia is approximately the size of the continental United States with only one-tenth the population. Most Australians live in urban centers near or on the coast. The outback is massive, with lots of desert and red rock and very few people.

After nearly three days of arduous travel (including layovers), I crawled out of the back of the dusty Cessna and ran to greet Louise. Even for a seasoned pilot, the journey was long. We hugged each other closely, or as close as you can get with two babies on the way! The years melted away. The line between mentor and mentee evaporated. Now seeing each other as grown women, each accomplished in our own right, we delighted in our reconnection.

Celebrating with birthday cake, good conversation, and long walks out on the station, Louise and I talked about our lives, my children, and hers that were soon to be born. We spoke about flying and what we had learned along the way. Louise thanked me again for demanding that she stay in her flight program. The relationship with the (then) boyfriend eventually ended. Without my push, she explained, she wouldn't have had her flying career. I was reminded that sometimes a mentor needs to encourage, and sometimes a mentor needs to give a big fat shove.

"One. More. Year!" I said with a wink. "I knew you could do it, even when you got distracted."

As we dove more deeply into her story, Louise shared that she had felt a bit lonely at times. "The [men] throughout my career were very supportive," she remarked. "I felt they looked after me and considered me one of the group, although different, if this makes sense. But I had to earn their respect both personally and skill wise."

"Being a woman in a male-dominated field, you have to do a good job, work hard and prove yourself—more so than a man," I agreed.

"In the Navy, we used to say that a woman walks into a squadron and has to prove she is a pilot. A man walks in, and it is assumed he is one."

Passion overcomes the challenges of being one of the few women in a male-dominated field. Louise had learned to shrug off comments from passengers who were surprised that she was the pilot. "Once you are in the air, it doesn't matter," she said, smiling.

Another lesson Louise learned was that being a woman—something she initially thought might be a weakness in her field—was actually a great strength in her career. "I had a point of difference," she said. "Generally speaking, women are very good at multitasking. I can fly a plane, run an office, and talk to customers and tourists very well." She spoke of one flying business based in central Australia that would only employ women pilots because of these abilities. She explained, "Not every hour of a pilot's career is flying. A point of difference is a huge benefit, for example, in an aviation tourism business."

Louise continued, "The women that I know who made it in aviation, we have a strong bond. We've worked hard and have been prepared to do all kinds of jobs. We are generally free-spirited, independent women." We both smiled. What I saw in Louise, she saw in me. She spoke of the importance of staying connected to these women, whether they be nearby or half a world away. For Louise, that was another woman pilot in Birdsville, a helicopter pilot in New Zealand, and me.

One morning as we sat on the back porch of her house, I looked out at the expanse of the land surrounding Pandie station. All I could see for miles was dusty, dry scrub. "How do you live here?" I asked. "How can anyone live here?" was what I was really thinking.

"We have everything we need," she explained. "The cattle eat the dry scrub, and they have enough water. The land gives them enough vitamins and minerals, so we don't have to provide supplemental feed.

We live on the Birdsville track that connects Birdsville to Adelaide nearly 1,500 kilometers away, and I get groceries delivered every week or two from Adelaide to my front door. It's really quite lovely." Where I saw nothingness, Louise saw opportunity.

Louise knew a lot about opportunities, seeing them as well as taking them. When I asked how she started her company, she explained that she had wanted to be an airline pilot and took a job in the outback to build her flight time. She had been flying "flat out"— eight hours a day, nearly seven days a week—for another company in Birdsville. She saw the demand for another company, a competitor. So she started Central Eagle Aviation with two Cessna 210 aircraft and some financing from her father. She was right. The demand was there, and customers kept coming. While I was in Birdsville, she took delivery of a fourth aircraft to cover the tourist rush. In 2011, Louise was selected as the Queensland Young Achiever of the Year.

Living in the outback presented other opportunities. She had become even more adept as a pilot and had learned to fix her own aircraft. Louise taught me that seeing and acting on opportunity is a skill that can be honed with practice, like a muscle built through lifting weights. Our dreams can change when we are open to the opportunities before us. Her dream changed from being an airline pilot to being a pilot in her own business.

EVEN WHEN OUR FLIGHT PLANS CHANGE, WE CAN STILL SOAR—AND PERHAPS EVEN HIGHER!

Even when our flight plans change, we can still soar—and perhaps even higher! I know that even when things do not work out as planned in our lives, new opportunities present themselves.

Aviators often talk of building situational awareness. Situational awareness means being acutely aware of the dynamic environment in which we operate. We have "good situational awareness" when we frequently study our instruments, check our mirrors, and scan the horizon outside the aircraft. "Bad situational awareness" occurs when we focus too intently on just one area or aspect of flying the plane. The results can be disastrous.

Build your situational awareness by directing your focus up and outward, actively looking for opportunities that exist in your environment, whether that be at your job, in school, in your network, or in your community. Of course, you do need to pay attention to the work or job directly in front of you. But when you become too narrowly focused on what is happening in front of you, you are likely to miss new and exciting prospects. Had Louise been focused solely on building flight hours to become an airline pilot, she might have missed the chance to start her own business.

Reconnecting with Louise turned out to be the best birthday gift I could have received. Her life experience reinforced so many lessons that I had learned throughout my life and career. She followed her dream, learned to look for opportunities, and grabbed them. I often remember Louise's words, "Up in the air ... it doesn't matter." No, it doesn't.

WHEN YOU DON'T FIT IN, CHOOSE TO STAND OUT

After several years as a business consultant in the aerospace sector, I felt a new calling for my life. My husband had decided he no longer wanted to be married, so I decided the time had come to reinvent myself. I packed up my grief along with my daughter (my son stayed with his father) and headed to Nashville, Tennessee, to begin a doctoral program in higher education, leadership, and policy at Vanderbilt University.

Although I entered the program with excellent credentials and outstanding experience, I found myself to be a bit of an oddity in my class, as I was the only one without formal experience in academia. I may have been a square peg in a round hole, but I had decades of experience as "the only" or "one of the only" in my Navy career. I joyously threw myself into the program, always remembering my well-traveled path of choosing to stand out when I didn't fit in.

The doctoral program was a perfect fit for me. My classmates were incredible professionals from all over the country. Their experience rubbed off on me, just as my experience rubbed off on them. After three years and many long hours, our capstone projects successfully defended, we graduated. I had completed yet another major milestone in my life and was ready for the next step on my journey. Fortunately, I didn't have to travel far this time.

My daughter and I had put down roots in Nashville. We had found community and a new rhythm in our lives. My passion for mentoring others, particularly young women, was rewarded when I accepted a position as the director of the Center for STEM Education for Girls at the Harpeth Hall School. My work in education became the new calling in my life.

As I transitioned into education, I remember walking into Harpeth Hall on my first official day. As I rounded the corner to my new office, my heart skipped a beat when I spied a historical WASP display inside a large glass case. Upon closer inspection, I discovered the story of WASP Cornelia Fort, a Nashville native and graduate of Ward-Belmont School, the predecessor school to Harpeth Hall.

As I read further, I learned that prior to joining the WASP, Cornelia had witnessed the bombing of Pearl Harbor. Already a pilot, she had been in the air flying with a student when she narrowly avoided a midair collision with a Japanese aircraft. After that experience, Cornelia knew she must assist with the war effort. She went on to join the Women's Auxiliary Ferrying Squadron (WAFS), then became a WASP when the two organizations merged.

WASP history in my new school … right outside my office! It felt like a sign, a confirmation that I was in the right place to begin my career in education. (During my time at Harpeth Hall, three young women accepted appointments to the US Naval Academy. Three in one year, in fact. Maybe they too needed to "see it to believe it.")

One of my favorite colleagues during my time at Harpeth Hall, and now a lifelong friend, was an English teacher named MarQuis. I was drawn to his classroom, as were others, because of the way he welcomed everyone who entered. At the beginning of each class period, MarQuis stood at the threshold of his classroom, always impeccably dressed, greeting each student by name. With a wave of his hand and a bright smile, the students were ushered into the room in a way they felt valued and seen. He made the space conducive to learning with yellow flowers adorning the tables and subtle music playing in the background. Everyone knew they were entering a special place of learning. In this space, students wrestled with classics like *The Secret Life of Bees, Fahrenheit 451*, and *A Raisin in the Sun* to learn about life, humanity, and who they want to be in the world.

Each time I entered MarQuis's classroom, I too felt the warmth of his welcome. One day I mentioned to him that I was writing this book about my experience in the Navy. "During my time at the Naval Academy, and then throughout my Navy career, I was often one of the few if not the only woman in anything I chose to do professionally. I knew I was always going to stand out. As I have gotten older, I have embraced the reality that standing out is actually an opportunity." He smiled with a knowing look of recognition in his eyes.

Fewer than 20 percent of the faculty at Harpeth Hall were men, and MarQuis was one of only two Black men at the all-girls school. We started at Harpeth Hall the same year as part of a cohort, and we connected immediately. He is a special man. I often wondered if he ever felt isolated.

One day I asked MarQuis about his experience as "one of the only." MarQuis shared that as a gay, Black man growing up in the South, he felt a sense of displacement. He said it did not help that he took piano lessons, played the violin, and longed to be as glamorous as Diana Ross, while his peers were into rap music and mainstream media. Similarly, most of his education had been in predominantly White schools, where he was often one of the few people of color, or the only one, in his advanced courses.

Then I asked him about the opportunities and benefits of choosing to stand out when you don't fit in, and this is what he said: "It took me a while, but I eventually came to learn that being different or standing out positioned me to be a change agent. I had a mentor who once said that most people continuously do what's already been done because they haven't encountered anyone brave enough to model other ways to show up, assume space, navigate, or make sense of the world. They haven't encountered a person brave enough to walk in the fullness of their power. By walking in my own power, I free others to walk in theirs. Showing up as my most authentic self has opened many doors academically and professionally. I offer a perspective that both enriches and complicates spaces, pushing my peers to expand their own beliefs regarding self and the world."

MarQuis suddenly made me realize that we women Naval aviators were change agents. It is obvious in hindsight, but until my conversation with him, I hadn't thought of it quite that way. By showing up as our authentic selves, we pushed others to expand their beliefs about what a woman could do in the Navy.

I AM CALLING YOU ... TO BE A CHANGE AGENT, A PIONEER, IN WHATEVER WAY YOU FEEL CALLED TO BE.

And that is what I am calling you to do—to be a change agent, a pioneer, in whatever way you feel called to be.

Although he is still young (not yet thirty), MarQuis is wise beyond his years. I am confident he will wear the mantle of school leadership one day. I imagine him stepping into the role of principal or head of school, or beyond. After his first two years at Harpeth Hall, he was awarded the Heath Jones Prize for the Promise of Excellence in Teaching. Then he saw the opportunity to become the director of equity and inclusion, and he jumped on it. MarQuis stands out, and MarQuis delivers.

When I think of a student who stands out, my thoughts immediately turn to Gracie. Gracie was a freshman at the time of this writing. She is beautiful, smart, and engaging and has cerebral palsy. Gracie has been through multiple surgeries since she was five years old to help her gain better control of her legs. Oftentimes she came to school either in a wheelchair, with a walker or using arm crutches. While one might think that Gracie stands out because of her disability, that is not what I see.

What makes Gracie exceptional is her spirit—her spirit of resilience, acceptance, and perseverance. Everyone knows Gracie because Gracie extends herself to everyone she comes in contact with, whether they are students, teachers, cafeteria workers, security guards, or the gentlemen who take care of the school grounds. She possesses a dazzling smile that says, "You matter to me."

During one term, I asked Gracie to come to my Introduction to Engineering class to be our resident expert for our Inclusive Design for Disabilities project. "Of course!" she responded gleefully. Gracie joined our class, told her story, and openly shared her struggles. Along the way, she suggested a few projects that the students might choose to make our campus more accessible for students like herself.

The students jumped at the opportunity to help Gracie. They designed prototype solutions to some of her challenges that we hoped the school would incorporate. A magical thing happened along the way. The students began to see our school campus through Gracie's eyes. They realized that leaving backpacks in the hallways was a barrier to access. Students who once complained about how hard it was to walk up the hill from the gym to the theater no longer complained. The change in the students was remarkable. Their whole perspective on access and inclusivity changed thanks to Gracie.

When you don't fit in, choose to stand out. And it is a choice.

For me, the turning point was my graduation from the Academy. I had been tested and tried, and no one could ever take away from me the fact that I was a graduate of the US Naval Academy and a woman graduate as well. When my Academy roommate Millie and I discussed this recently, she concurred. "It's a choice how to view standing out in a group when you don't fit in. It requires confidence in yourself when no one else has it. It pushes you to perform better, to look better, to work harder."

Because of my experiences, I have a heart for those who put themselves in positions where they know they will stand out. Their stories inspire me. It takes courage to be in the minority, chosen or unchosen.

Standing out is an opportunity, an opportunity to grow more fully into who we have been called to be and to be a change maker for our world. Be brave, stand out, and make your presence known.

NEW HORIZONS

A few years ago, I got word that one of my role models and colleagues was nearing the end of her life. Captain Rosemary Mariner was the first Navy woman jet pilot and became the "point woman" for opening up military aviation to women. She lived near Knoxville, Tennessee, so I made the trip from Nashville to see her in her last days.

Rosemary and I met in the mideighties. I had known of her by reputation and, as a young aviator, looked forward to meeting her. While in California for training, I called her and went over to her squadron to introduce myself. Our mutual regard for one another began that day.

While petite in stature, Rosemary had the strength and determination of a giant. She understood that what she was doing was far bigger than herself. As point woman, she encouraged, prodded, and pushed us to create our own career paths, similar to the men. While many people liked her, many men, particularly the "good old boys," hated her because she challenged the status quo. She was the fly in the ointment, the woman intent on rocking the boat. Remember, it was Rosemary who led the charge to repeal the combat exclusion laws. She knew we must resist, and resist we did.

It was a privilege to be able to say goodbye to Rosemary and to thank her in person for her impact on my Navy career. Sitting at her bedside, I leafed through the articles I brought about our time on Capitol Hill. We spoke of the work she inspired. We smiled, recognizing that since our work together decades earlier, a new generation of women military aviators had taken over.

The WASP are now called the "first wave" of women military aviators. Rosemary and I are part of the "second wave," which includes the women who started flying in the seventies until 1993 when the combat exclusion laws were repealed. We are currently in the "third wave" of women military aviators. They are the women who fly everything the military possesses, on any type of mission. The girls and young women I have the opportunity to teach and speak to are the "fourth wave." It will be incredibly exciting to see what they accomplish as their futures unfold. Perhaps they will be the first women to pilot a spacecraft to Mars.

Although she died young at the age of sixty-five, Rosemary's influence will continue for decades to come. Those final moments we shared together were sacred, and I will treasure them always.

At Rosemary's memorial, I spent time with women from several decades of my Navy life. I embraced women I had not seen since the eighties, met other women who were Rosemary's peers, and saw my dearest women aviator friends. After the church service, we headed to the graveside service where Rosemary would be given full military honors. The honor guard fired their rifles, signaling the beginning of the ceremony. As the chaplain finished his message, the honor guard removed the flag draped over her coffin, ceremoniously folded it, and gave it to her family with the words: "On behalf of the President of the United States, the United States Navy, and a grateful nation, please accept this flag as a symbol of our appreciation for your loved one's honorable and faithful service."

I, too, was grateful for Rosemary and her service.

Then the most amazing thing happened.

From the east, a flight of four F/A-18s with *entirely female crews* appeared on the horizon, headed in our direction. It was the missing man formation. Or might I say this time, the missing woman formation! This formation is an aerial salute performed at a funeral, typically in memory of a fallen aviator. Four planes fly in a formation with a space where a fifth plane should be, symbolizing the person's absence. As the missing woman formation flew directly overhead, one aircraft peeled off and headed directly up toward the heavens, as the rest of the aircraft continued in formation in level flight.

I cried out both in sadness and exhilaration. They were all women aviators! It was a profound moment for all of us and an incredibly fitting final sign of respect for Rosemary.

At the reception that followed, I met the all-female crews that had flown the F/A-18s. What they said will stick in my memory forever: no one had ever told them no. After forty-five years, our collective work had finally come to this: all women have now been completely accepted in the United States Navy as aviators and equals. The flyover tribute the

ALL WOMEN HAVE NOW BEEN COMPLETELY ACCEPTED IN THE UNITED STATES NAVY AS AVIATORS AND EQUALS.

Navy paid to Rosemary signaled a seismic shift in Naval Aviation. We rightly honored Rosemary as a pioneer, and by extension, we also honored all our women aviators—past, present, and future.[21]

The change that has transpired in the Navy over the last several decades mirrors what has transpired in other fields previously dominated by men. My story is not unique. It mirrors the stories of other brave and courageous women in other fields who have challenged the status quo, refused to be dismissed, and made the decision to be different and stand out. Today, women are leading countries, leading Fortune 50 companies and leading their families and communities. But there is still more work to be done.

Each of us—you and me—are part of the story, a story that will continue to unfold for years to come. It is the story that must live on, the story which links one generation to the next as we press ever forward in the world.

When I hit a wall,
I am going to get under it,
over it or around it.

—CAPTAIN ROSEMARY MARINER

First woman to command a military aviation squadron

---

21   Based on my op-ed submitted to Knox News, "Capt. Rosemary Mariner Was a Leader among Leaders | Opinion," https://www.knoxnews.com/story/opinion/2019/03/04/ captain-rosemary-mariner-leader-naval-aviator-pioneer/2916772002/.

FIND YOUR WINGS

B elow are some questions to get you thinking about where you are now and where you want to go in the future. My hope is that these thought starters will help you identify your goals and dreams and chart a course to achieve them. Visit www.captainbarbarabell.com to download a free tool to help you create your own "flight plan."

WHO IS IN YOUR PAST AND PRESENT?

Remember you are not alone. Others have gone before you, and others will follow. Who are the successful women in your industry that you can seek out as a mentor?

STEP OUT ON FAITH.

Is there an opportunity in your life that you have been hesitant to move forward with because you think you have to know every step you will need to take before you get started? It is time to step out on faith and get going. Take the first step, and see where it takes you. Then take the next step and the next, and you'll be surprised where you end up!

ARE YOU CLIPPING YOUR OWN WINGS?

Have you convinced yourself that you do not have what it takes to accomplish your goals? Do you tell yourself you'll get back to your dream "someday"? It is all too easy to find a "legitimate reason" (i.e., an excuse) to keep your dream on the shelf. You owe it to yourself to make you and your dreams your number-one priority. What one action, no matter how small, can you take today to get your dream back on track?

BUILD SITUATIONAL AWARENESS.

Is your focus too narrow? What opportunities might you be missing that could move you toward your goals?

WHAT DO YOU CHOOSE?

Do you feel "different" from those around you? Choose today to stand out. Decide to be your authentic self and walk in your power. What can you do to set the example and be a role model for those women coming behind you? What skills or life experiences do you have to share that could benefit other women? Be that change agent who will inspire someone else.

There's something straight in the way
she stands that says she's seen
what the world looks like from the clouds.

—SHERRI L. SMITH

from *Flygirl*

THE MAGIC OF FLIGHT

Recently a colleague asked, "Do you remember the first time you flew?"

Initially I spontaneously told him, "No." But then that simple question spurred wonderful memories from many years ago and feelings of nostalgia from my first flight.

As I mentioned earlier, I took flight lessons to earn my private pilot's license while at the Naval Academy. As background, when my brother was at the Air Force Academy, my parents offered that they would pay for flying lessons if he wanted to take them. Dan never took them up on their offer. Cleverly figuring that what was offered to one child was available to the others, I decided to take flying lessons. One day I called my parents and told them I was going to take them up on their offer.

"What offer?" they said with a note of confusion in their voices.

"Thanks for offering to pay for flying lessons," I said gleefully. "You made the offer to Dan, so I know it is open to me as well." A bit perplexed, they grudgingly agreed.

As a first-class midshipman (senior) at the Naval Academy, I joined the Naval Academy Flying Club with my friend Lisa, the same woman who became my roommate in Pensacola. We took ground school, jammed between dinner and study hours. Later we squeezed in flight time after classes and on the weekends.

I fondly remember my first flight. After briefing our flight in the trailer that was the headquarters for our flying club, I anxiously stepped outside with my instructor. Off in the distance, I spotted the Cessna that would take me into the air. "Ah yes, here we go!" I bubbled inside.

We walked around the aircraft, inspecting the flight control surfaces, the engine, the tires and brakes, the fuel and oil status, and the surface of the propeller. After climbing into the plane, we performed our preflight checks. Then I semicalmly started the engine, and the propeller sputtered to life. As I rocked back and forth with the vibration of the engine, adrenaline began to flood my body. I radioed the control tower for clearance to taxi. Then, bumping and squeaking along, we taxied from the grass onto the taxiway, holding short of the runway to do our engine and flight control checks.

The instructor asked me to follow the motions of his hands on the dual yoke of the aircraft. We radioed the tower for clearance to take off, and before I knew it, we began to roll forward. Turning onto the runway, we advanced to full throttle and released the brakes. As the Cessna rumbled down the runway, my excitement amplified. We began to feel lighter in our seats, and then it happened—the moment of lift—we were airborne!

I call it the magic of flight.

The gravitational forces that held us back and held us on the ground were overcome by our own forward momentum and the lift created by air rushing over our wings.

There is a great life lesson in the aerodynamics of flight.

What are the forces that are holding you down and holding you back? What is keeping you from getting off the ground and soaring in your life and in your career? When you hear in your head, "I couldn't possibly do that," you clip your own wings. You restrict your own potential and limit how high you can fly.

Don't have the education or skills you need? Go get them! Seek out professional development opportunities to build your skills. Community college might be a great start for education. Think you are too old to start school? I went back to school at fifty-three. I have a friend who started at seventy-two. You are never too old.

Afraid to change majors or switch jobs? Find a mentor to guide and advise you. Sometimes we think we have to have everything planned out before we commit. We don't. Just take the first step, then the next and the next. Practice making small changes, and the big ones will become less scary.

Know that failure is inevitable at some point. Aviators train extensively to handle failure—engine failure, electrical systems failure, navigation systems failure—because they know it is not a matter of *if*, but *when* a problem will occur during flight. We train for countless hours in simulators to know how to handle those failures when they happen. Learn from your mistakes and get back in the air. We often learn more from flying through turbulence than from a smooth, easy flight.

And finally, remember that flight plans change. Life will throw some unexpected situations your way. I recently left my job as the director of the Center for STEM Education for Girls at Harpeth Hall for new adventures at Vanderbilt University and another phase of my career. Sometimes we need to adjust our dreams and goals. Simply set your course for a new destination and continue on.

> **SOMETIMES WE NEED TO ADJUST OUR DREAMS AND GOALS. SIMPLY SET YOUR COURSE FOR A NEW DESTINATION AND CONTINUE ON.**

Finding your wings and rising to the top takes hard work, endurance, and persistence. You have to be in it for the long haul. Know why you are where you are, and what you are there to do. Then get busy. Whenever we create forward motion in our lives, we generate the lift that will take us to new heights.

I have had the opportunity to experience life in the third dimension—flying up high in the air. It is an experience beyond all others. What I feel in the air is a sense of freedom that traces all the way back to the dreams I had as a child—the sense of loosening your ties to the earth and soaring. Looking down on the earth, then up at the vast sky, you feel part of something much bigger than yourself, while also feeling that you are just one small speck in the universe.

Your perspective changes, forever.

That is my hope for you—that you will learn to fly in your life and career and have that same perspective-changing experience. When you find your wings and soar, it is a feeling like no other.

And you are ready. You are cleared for takeoff. Run up your engines, release the brakes that are slowing you down, and accelerate down the runway. Your future awaits on the horizon. It's time to find your wings … and soar!

PHOTOS

USNA Induction day

USNA Graduation day

Navy Captain photo

Louise and me at Birdsville AU

Incoming Change of Command

Celebrating retirement with the sisterhood

Flying in Germany

Flying an F-16

My good friend JR Brown and his daughter Jocelyn, whom I inspired to go to TPS

*At the PAX River Aviation Museum's "Women
in Aviation" exhibit opening*

Heading out for a flight at Test Pilot School

Retirement day with Admiral Smiley Enewold presiding

Retirement day, speaking my final words of reflection

ABOUT THE AUTHOR

Growing up in a small town in Michigan, Barbara Bell, Ed.D., Captain U.S. Navy (ret), had her head in the clouds. "As a kid, lying on the grass, seeing planes go by, I wasn't thinking about being a pilot, because there was no context for that for women in the 1960s," she remembers. "When I dreamed of flying, I was always the airplane."

An accomplished student and athlete, she received an appointment to the U.S. Naval Academy at a time when only 6 percent of the student body was female. After becoming one of Annapolis's first woman graduates, she continued on to a distinguished career as an aviator and Naval Flight Test Officer, during which she flew more than 1,600 hours in 35 different types of U.S. and Allied aircraft. In 1992, she and fellow aviators went to Capitol Hill to successfully repeal the combat exclusions laws, opening up combat aircraft and ships to women in the services. She is happy to report that women now fly unrestricted in the services.

Today, Bell draws upon the skills she developed throughout her trailblazing years of service to help others find the courage to test new and innovative ways of thinking and doing. Using her principles of values-based leadership, she's become known for her empathy, as well as her ability to ignite the spark people need to envision their dreams and chart a path forward.

She pairs that practical side with plenty of inspiration, thanks to her belief in tackling challenges from a higher perspective. "I see the world so differently as a result of flying," she says, with trademark passion. "I understand that sense of adventure: building up speed, and then the moment of lift. That sense of being *up*. It's like a whole new world. I've lived and flown in all three dimensions."

Dr. Bell holds a B.S. in systems engineering from the United States Naval Academy, an M.S. in astronautical engineering from the Naval Postgraduate School, an M.A. in theology from Marylhurst University, and a doctorate in education from Vanderbilt University and is a graduate of Navy Test Pilot School. She is dedicated to preparing the next generation of leaders for our world.

ACKNOWLEDGMENTS

This process of writing this book has required a long, deep dive into the inner sanctum of my life. So many of you have helped along the way and to you I owe a great debt of gratitude.

First I start with Jacob Stuart, who challenged me with his words, "You must write your book and I will give you the name of the woman who will help you do so." Your words felt like a lightning bolt message from God above that the time had come to take the message I had spoken for so many years, and turn my story into this book.

To Wendy Kurtz at Elizabeth Charles and Associates who IS that woman who made my book a reality. Starting with our first strategy session, I knew Wendy and her editor Juli Baldwin were the perfect match for me. Wendy, you challenged, coached and pushed me to go deeper into myself to access my story in new way. Through countless hours of draft development, editing and always telling me to "add more emotion!" you and Juli picked me up when I hit the ground knowing all along that you would bring out the best in me. You did and I thank you.

To my dear friend SaraLyn Archibald, granddaughter of WASP Betty Archibald, thank you for bringing our friendship to a whole new level. Through your expertise as a theater teacher, you helped me bring a range of emotions—joy, sadness, anger and exhilaration—into this work and into my life. You have true WASP DNA. Never forget that!

And to author and dear friend Molly Davis, you taught me much about the process of writing and so much more about the process of becoming more of who I am and how I want to be in this world. Your books *Letters to Our Daughters* (written along with Kristine Van Raden) and *Blush* taught me that writing from the heart matters most.

To my many friends whom I consider family, you have been my key encouragers through my entire adult life. From my USNA roommates Millie and Karen, to my closest Navy colleagues including J.R. Brown and my dearest friend Harry Robinson, you have served as ongoing witnesses to my life. You were there from the beginning to the end of my naval career and continue to be an ever-present force in my life. While I cannot name everyone who influenced me during my career in the Navy, you get the call out this time.

To my all friends in Nashville, Jo and Jimmy in particular. Jo, you wrote with me at the coffee shop when this was book was merely an outline and cheered me on through our weekly breakfast meetings at Thistle Farms Café. Jimmy, you encouraged me as both a friend and as a single parent—and then created an incredible website to frame my work!

To my brothers Jim and Dan, and my recently departed mom and dad, you have been there from the beginning. Thank you.

And finally, to my team at Advantage|ForbesBooks. You took

the manuscript Wendy and I delivered several months ago, sculpted it with your incredible expertise, wrapped it in a beautiful cover and launched it into the atmosphere. Let's fly high!

SERVICES

Looking for your next inspiring keynote speaker? Or for ways to improve both your personal leadership and team performance? Barbara can help you.

Whether you have a large group or a small team, want on-site training, or need to deliver programs to multiple locations simultaneously, Barbara has a variety of formats and delivery capabilities to fit your needs and budget. Her programs can be customized to meet your unique goals and objectives.

Barbara also speaks regularly at local, regional and national events and conferences. Her programs are highly rated by participants and meeting planners alike.

Connect with Barbara at CaptainBarbaraBell.com. Follow her on Linked In at https://www.linkedin.com/in/barbara-bell-ed-d/; Instagram at @captainbarbarabell; or Twitter at @captbarbarabell.

CPSIA information can be obtained
at www.ICGtesting.com
Printed in the USA
LVHW022206041022
729958LV00001B/155